CW00820621

OPUS 111

Vicente Aboites

MINERVA PRESS
MONTREUX LONDON WASHINGTON

ISBN 1 85863 705 8

First Published 1996 by
MINERVA PRESS
195 Knightsbridge
London SW7 1RE

Printed in Great Britain by
B.W.D. Ltd., Northolt, Middlesex

OPUS 111

Translated from the Spanish by Jacqueline Burke

OPUS 111

Years of dreams, years of work, years of youthful illusions seemed finally to have crystallised. The time that had passed between the passionate reading of childhood and adolescence – *The Double Helix, The Microbe Hunters*, and others – and this moment seemed, now, diminutive, although she alone could know, for having experienced it, the true extent of the time and effort involved.

Telegram in hand, she jumped with unbridled joy. She had read it innumerable times and, in spite of the cold and bureaucratic language, it seemed to her written in the most exquisite prose although it only read: "*Srta*. Helena Ibargüengoitia, File No. 1728. Grant to pursue doctoral studies in Cambridge, England, approved. Present yourself at this office as quickly as possible to sign appropriate forms. Grants Office, CONACYT."

The following days were full of feverish activity. There were visits to the British Council and the British Embassy, medical examinations, a whole day spent queuing at the Office of Foreign Affairs to obtain a passport; making the arrangements to leave the guest house where she had been lodging, as well as choosing some books and notes that she considered useful, packing up the rest of her books, clothes and personal belongings and sending them to her parents' house in Guanajuato. There, of course, some family farewell parties had already been arranged. Naturally, with so much activity, she felt a little bewildered but radiant with happiness.

The farewell at the airport of Mexico City was very emotional. Her father embraced her, saying, "Helena, look after yourself and write us frequently with your news; after all I'm getting on a bit and possibly may never see you again..."

Once on the aeroplane, she couldn't help shedding a few tears. She thought tenderly of her sister, her brother, her parents; she remembered their childhood games, which were now so far away. It seemed to be a magical thing that that slim girl with large black eyes had been transformed into a young woman of twenty-four who was setting forth on her own to see the world. From the moment she left her home at the age of eighteen to study biology in Morelia and later travelled to Mexico to take her masters in genetics and molecular biology, she had visited her parents' home so seldom that she had gained the reputation of being "hard", "distant", although the truth was quite to the contrary. Visiting her parents and then having to say goodbye depressed her so much that she chose to visit them only occasionally.

After a stop in New York, the British Airways Boeing 747 continued its nine hour journey to London. She had spent days in extreme excitement, and took advantage of the opportunity to sleep a little. However, she woke up well before the descent and spent a long time watching the cumulus clouds, which seemed more like enormous pieces of cotton, until, between the gaps in the clouds, she was able to see the immense blue of the sea and saw for the first time the British coast line. Her emotions were indescribable.

In spite of her being of mixed ethnic origin, like most Mexicans, almost all her education – at school, but above all, at home – had been based on European cultural values. The majority of the poets and novelists that she loved, she had read and re-read, first with her parents and then alone. Those that had most left a mark on her spirit, were European; the same with painters, sculptors, composers and philosophers that had taken her to ecstasy a thousand and one times since her childhood, and, of course, the scientists that she esteemed the most were European. Coming to Europe meant living the adventure of rediscovering a fundamental part of her cultural roots. To live on the same continent, in the same atmosphere as practically all the individuals that she admired for their intellectual creativity, was little short of the miraculous. It meant returning to the cradle of her culture. Her heart pounded.

She passed through customs without any problems and, as a gesture of courtesy, she received a small folder which included maps and tourist information about Great Britain that she found immediately useful for taking the underground to Liverpool Street and from there the train to Cambridge.

Throughout the whole journey she couldn't help noticing how formally the majority of the British people dressed: men, women, children and young people. Black suits, grey suits, black skirts, grey skirts, white blouses, blue blouses, striped shirts, ties, umbrellas, newspapers – oh, so many newspapers!

The Times, *The Daily Telegraph*, *The Guardian*, *The Sun* etc. etc. – and the pointed shoes worn by ninety per cent of the women. For a moment she couldn't help avoiding the sensation that she was in the offices of a Mexican bank, although the silence and politeness of the people, only disturbed by the monotonous rhythm of the wheels of the train, clearly reminded her of the alien environment.

The landscape, entirely uneventful, made an impression on her. Everything was plain, plain, plain, sometimes interrupted by gentle hills. All the tones of green were present; the grass was emerald and the trees were the colour of algae, blended with a sunless sky, although equally rich in tones of blue and grey and all at the same time immersed in a light haze.

On arriving in Cambridge she took a taxi to the accommodation office to pick up the keys of the flat which they had reserved for her and which, as they explained, she would be sharing with two other students who weren't there at that moment. She spent a good while unpacking and putting her clothes away. She had almost finished when she heard the main door open: it was Nancy, a North American student, who had recently arrived and who – she found out later – was studying for her masters in literature that year.

It was almost dusk when they decided to go out to a local pub where Helena hungrily devoured a ham-and-cheese filled baked potato and drank a pint of dark warmish beer that she didn't like at first, but as Nancy explained to her, "The English believe that this is the most suitable drink to accompany a cold wet day... which means all the time!"

On returning to the flat they met James, the third flatmate, an Englishman who was doing his doctorate in pure mathematics. And the truth was that given his appearance, it would have been difficult to have imagined him dedicating himself to anything else. He greeted them politely and then immediately shut himself into his room. Nancy and Helena decided to have a cup of tea before going to bed, and they chatted about the little they knew of life in Cambridge.

The following day Helena introduced herself to Professor Emil Jackson in the university laboratory of molecular biology. Professor Jackson, whom she knew through his scientific articles, would from now on be her doctoral supervisor. He took her round the laboratories, showing her all the equipment and at the same time introducing her to the other members of the research team. Helena was deeply impressed by the layout, by the vast amount of apparatus of the laboratories and the way it was all set up, as well as by the friendliness and politeness of Professor Jackson. They spent several hours in discussion. Helena explained to him the details of the research which she had carried out whilst studying for her masters in Mexico and also talked about the articles she was working on. He in his turn went into some detail about specific aspects of her work and, taking into consideration what she knew already about certain experimental techniques, suggested to her some lines of investigation. Finally, he gave her a bundle of some fifty or sixty articles which she had to study carefully as soon as possible. Then he showed her to her work station and desk.

After this long conversation she went to her work station, sat down euphorically, and alone, in front of her desk, immediately began to work.

During the following weeks, apart from going through the enrolment procedures, she concentrated on her work, spending at least twelve hours a day on it, interrupted only by lunch-time at one o'clock and dinner at six. She got to know her companions at the other lab benches, students who were also doing their doctorates. There was Peter, an English fellow, who was very serious and wore a perpetual frown, and Marwan, a Kurd from Iraq, who was very tall and rather shy, but who always maintained a slight smile on his face, evidence, as Helena was later to become aware of daily, of his enormous inclination to help others.

In the evenings, she went to a pub with Nancy – always a different one – although it seemed that Nancy had already toured them all. Or else she read her edition of *Hamlet* with a commentary, published by the University of Cambridge, which she had recently bought. She had always deeply enjoyed it but, finding herself in England, regarded it as almost a moral obligation to re-read it in a good edition.

The conversations she had with Nancy were limited to daily events and so were very superficial. In spite of the fact that at the beginning she had been pleased to know her, it didn't take her long to realise that their relationship was condemned to remain banal and superficial. On one occasion in a pub, Helena, trying to steer the conversation away from trivial things towards literature, asked Nancy what she thought of the work of Balzac, Zola and Hugo; she replied that she had not heard of either of the first two and that she had never read Victor Hugo. And in fact, she wasn't interested in doing so. She was interested solely in writers who wrote in English, and she considered that the richness of literature in English was more than enough. Helena asked her if she didn't think it a little strange that a person could go by the title of philosopher and yet has never read Hegel, Kant or Marx. Nancy assured her that she didn't understand the question as, although she had never heard of the first two persons named, she hadn't understood the relationship between a communist like Marx and a philosopher. Without any more comment, Helena carried on talking about the outlandish punks that crowded the streets and the pubs.

She was fascinated by Cambridge; its narrow streets and sombre buildings delighted her as much as the green countryside around the city. For a few pounds she bought a second-hand bicycle on which she made long trips of three hours or more during the weekends. Feeling the freedom of the country, the air, the dew from the mist and frequent drops of rain on her face took her back to her childhood. Doubtless, this was one of the aspects of her stay in England which she enjoyed enormously; the other was not having to use make-up. She had never liked making her face up, and in Mexico they had made her feel that she didn't quite fit in without it, whereas here in England, with or without make-up, she was just another young female student lost in her anonymity.

In the following weeks she tried to get an appointment with Professor Jackson without any success. When he did finally find the time, the interview was so short and unsatisfactory that Helena wasn't even able to express the basic ideas of her interpretation of the problem in which she was deeply engaged. Several weeks later the same thing happened again. On one occasion when she was preparing some demonstrations in the laboratory, Marwan happened to be there at the same time, and in the ensuing chat they compared notes about their difficulties in getting a decent interview with Professor Jackson. Marwan smiled and said, "Of course he's not going to discuss every little detail that happens to occur to you."

"But these things are important; they're the basis of what is going to be my thesis," interrupted Helena.

Marwan replied, "Your thesis matters to nobody – least of all to him. What interests him is that you get results from your investigation that can be published. When you have an article ready, without forgetting, of course, to include his name in the text and references, then you can discuss it with him – if he has time, of course. If not, well, you can send it for publication anyway. I know people who, throughout their entire research, have had only one or even no useful meetings with him."

Helena, disconcerted, asked, "But how can that happen?"

"It can happen," said Marwan, "because this laboratory here is one of the most prestigious in the world. The teachers need us as labour to publish and contribute to their scientific prestige and to that of the laboratory. They don't value us for taking their time up. Have you ever thought of the number of young scientists who would envy your place in this laboratory? Well, that has its price."

Helena remained puzzled by this conversation and for the rest of the day and the following week continued to think about it. She realised that to expect a kind of academic paternalism like you get in Mexico was senseless, and so, following the advice of Marwan, she tried to attend as many meetings as she could that were relevant to her subject, where she would have the opportunity of getting to know about the latest scientific results in her field of study, as well as being able to discuss them with other researchers and to confirm or reject her own ideas.

At the same time she became aware that to Professor Jackson, and to nearly all the other teachers, it was all the same whether she or any other foreign student took one, five or ten years to complete their doctorate, given that the award was granted exclusively for results obtained and not for a specific period of study.

Helena regarded the situation as a challenge. From then on she spent twelve to fifteen hours working daily, interrupted only by mealtimes and the little half-hour run that she did every day after getting up at seven o'clock. Marwan, on the other hand, in fact slept in the laboratory – not more than about three to five hours a day – and worked the rest of the time.

In her conversations with Marwan, Helena began to perceive the reasons for this behaviour. Marwan belonged to a group that was persecuted and discriminated against in Iraq: he was Kurdish, and a few months previously he had been informed, without any proper explanation, that his grant was being withdrawn in twelve months' time. Besides, in Helena's opinion, the denigrating and at times frankly humiliating treatment given to him by his Iraqi fellow students – who were not of Kurdish origin – contributed greatly to the pressure upon Marwan. She had often noticed how they irritated him with questions to the point of confusing him and making him look ridiculous. The empathy between Helena and Marwan increased, as did their scientific collaboration, and this was a great help as she was able to do in weeks what otherwise would have taken her months.

In six weeks of intense work they obtained sufficient results to prepare a paper for the International Congress of Molecular Biology that was to take place in London. And this was in spite of the subtle but tenacious boycott to which they were subjected by Peter, their laboratory colleague, who, on the pretext of needing some equipment or instrument which they happened to be using at that very moment, took it even though it was being used in some quantifying exercise. This caused them a great deal of annoyance as it meant that they had to start all over again. The relationship between Peter and Helena had been cold, and with these sorts of incidents it became, frankly, hostile. From the moment that they had been introduced Helena sensed something about Peter, above all when he commented, "Ah! You're from Mexico, that third-world country in South America, a neighbour of Brazil, isn't it?"

One night, after finishing some observations with the microscope, Helena was getting ready to leave when, on entering Marwan's work station, she discovered him, seated at his table, self-absorbed and looking at a chessboard. Given the great activity that was typical of Marwan, Helena found it surprising to find him in such a situation, even a little comic, and she couldn't help laughing.

"Come on, play a game with me, please," said Marwan, on hearing Helena.

"Well, O.K., although I'm a very bad player," answered Helena, still recovering from her surprise.

As a little girl she had learned to play chess with her father and now, faced with this situation, she was glad she had done so. In spite of the fact that she was not at all an exceptional player, she noticed that Marwan was making moves on the board which were totally incomprehensible, so she said to him, "I'm a bad player, but I'm sure that you can play a lot better than you're doing at the moment... I think that you're very distracted. You're tired, aren't you?"

"Yes," answered Marwan in an unnaturally serious manner.

This was all very strange. The scene ceased to be amusing for Helena, who got the feeling that Marwan had a problem.

"What's the matter with you? You seem to be tired, preoccupied, distracted – or all three at once."

"Yes, I do feel a little ill."

"You should leave your work as it is, go to your room and have a good sleep and forget about your bed in the laboratory and everything else for today. Would you like a beer? Maybe it would make you feel better."

"No, no. Come back to my room with me. I'd rather chat."

At that point in the conversation Helena noticed that there was something the matter with Marwan psychologically. She went with him to his room where they had a conversation which surprised Helena as much by the fact that Marwan's eyes were sometimes tearful as by the fact that the thread of his conversation lacked its usual coherence. He spoke of his people, the Kurds, of his family, his girlfriend, and of his university studies in Iraq. When Helena felt that he was a little calmer, she decided to take her leave as she, too, felt tired. Marwan, weeping, begged her not to leave him alone and said that she could borrow his sleeping bag to spend the night there, but not to leave him there alone because he was afraid of being murdered.

"Who wants to kill you?" asked Helena, totally mystified.

Marwan was not able to respond to this question, but from what he then said, Helena realised that Marwan's fear had no real foundation; it was purely the product of his imagination. It was by now almost four o'clock in the morning, so after settling Marwan in, she got into the sleeping bag and, although she was very perplexed about the whole matter, managed to fall asleep immediately.

Helena woke Marwan up early, they had a light breakfast and then, on the insistence of Helena, went to the medical clinic. Marwan only allowed himself to be examined on the condition that Helena was present. Once she was in the room, the doctor asked him, "What's the problem?"

"Ask Helena, she knows."

Helena, surprised by Marwan's answer and the strangeness of the situation, only managed to say a little worriedly, "Well, I think

Marwan is very tired from overworking... perhaps a few vitamins might help him..."

The doctor listened to her without taking his eyes off Marwan, who was staring into space, and then asked him, "How do you feel? What's worrying you?"

"They want to kill me," was Marwan's disconcerting reply.

"Who wants to kill you?"

"Everybody, they are all after me and they want to kill me," said Marwan, getting more and more agitated.

At that moment the doctor stopped the inquisitive interrogation and adopted a tone that was slower and more paternal. "Now, take it easy, take it easy. We don't want to harm you, we only want to help you. Why not tell us about the time you first realised that they were out to kill you?"

The doctor, at the same time as he made discreet signals to Helena to act normally, was dialling a telephone number. A few minutes later an ambulance arrived, and the doctor, interrupting Marwan, said, "I think that you have been subjected to a lot of stress and overwork. These people – and he indicated the nurses from the ambulance who were standing in the doorway – will take you to a hospital where you will be able to rest and relax for a few days."

"No!" shouted Marwan. "They are going to kill me. I'm not leaving here unless Helena comes with me."

"Calm down, Marwan," interrupted Helena. "They won't hurt you. I'll go to the hospital with you."

The ambulance took them to a psychiatric hospital. Once there, Helena calmed him down and was only able to leave him by promising to visit him the next day.

*****

Helena went back to the laboratory to work and to prepare some slides for the paper she was giving the following week at the International Congress of Molecular Biology in London. She felt confused and concerned about Marwan. She finished work early and shut herself in her room to read and listen to Mozart.

Early the following morning she bought some flowers and went to see Marwan. A nurse took her to the hospital ward which was dark and depressing, more like a prison. There, in a long, narrow room containing five beds with a small window at the far end, she found Marwan in the last bed.

Helena paused in the doorway to greet him; she smiled broadly, waving the flowers. Suddenly she froze, as if electrified. Marwan stared blankly and made incomprehensible gestures; he did not recognise her. He was scarcely able to utter any words through the saliva that dribbled from his mouth. She just dropped the flowers and started to cry. The nurse led her away and stayed with her as she wept inconsolably. She explained to her that, given the seriousness of Marwan's condition, they had to sedate him considerably, and he was still suffering from the effects. They suggested she come back in a few days, by which time he should be recuperated. As the congress in London was to begin in a few days, Helena decided to come back when it was over.

She went back to the laboratory feeling depressed and carried on preparing material for both herself and Marwan for the conference. The following Monday morning she left for London.

Once there, she realised for the first time that she had already been in England for several months but had done practically no sightseeing except in Cambridge and the surrounding area, but had immersed herself in her experiments to the point of obsession. The temperature during those days varied between eight and fifteen degrees. The trees had already lost their leaves. She heard on the news that the first snow had fallen in Scotland. She was fascinated by the colours of the countryside, and she enjoyed the fresh air enormously, as she felt it made the skin of her face and body feel smoother and fresher than ever.

She stayed in a small hotel near Piccadilly, and from there she made her way to Queen Mary College where all the sessions of the conference were taking place. At the inaugural session of the congress, she got to know many young research students like herself, ranging from those who, by their manner of speech, dress and behaviour, stood out as venerable professors, to those whom you could mistake for rockers or punks. There were research students there from the entire so-called First World.

Helena found the sessions very interesting, but exhausting. Fortunately the programme included some sightseeing trips, and she went on all of them. So she visited the Houses of Parliament, saw Big Ben and Buckingham Palace, and went for a trip along the Embankment.

She felt nervous about presenting her paper. It was going to be the first time that she had used English to address an audience of specialists. As far as language was concerned, she soon stopped worrying as, after listening to the Japanese struggling to produce an almost incomprehensible English, she realised that she would have no problems in expressing herself adequately. As far as the specialists were concerned, she also stopped worrying as she realised that her paper was comparable to, or more interesting and original than those which had already been presented. At the break, after she had delivered her paper, a professor from the University of Paris came up to her and commented on her conclusions, which he had thought worthy of note. He invited her to visit his institute the following week to give a talk about her work.

"You speak French, of course? It would be better if you did."

"*Oui, Professeur Bergé, je parle Français,*" replied Helena, thinking how grateful she was to her father who had encouraged her to study languages.

That evening, on a tour of London's evening spots with a group of research students of various nationalities, she found out that several others had been given invitations by professors to visit their laboratories.

"Of course!" said one of them who was Dutch, "For a research group co-ordinated by a professor, the best way of knowing what other groups are doing is not only to read the scientific articles that they publish, but to invite young researchers like ourselves who, partly through vanity, interest or innocence, are willing to talk in great detail about the work that they are undertaking in their laboratories."

"Exactly," interjected a young Swedish woman, "but what else can we do? These are the opportunities that we have to show our capabilities and to establish the relations that, as professionals, are necessary to us."

A student called Philippe, on finding out that Helena had been invited to Paris by Professor Bergé, was kind enough to offer her lodging in his home for the three days of her stay. Helena readily accepted and thanked him, mainly because four months had passed and she had not received her grant from CONACYT and was living off her savings, so saving the expense of three nights in a hotel didn't seem a bad idea.

At the end of the conference she decided to spend the weekend in London. She visited the National Gallery and the Tate Gallery where she spent many rapturous hours admiring the pictures that from an early age she had seen in her father's books: Durer, Cranach, Rembrandt, Van Gogh, Matisse, Monet, Renoir, Picasso, Klee, Ernst... it happened on more than one occasion that she was so absorbed she forgot the time and remained contemplating a picture until the dampness on her cheeks brought her back to reality.

She also attended a concert at the Royal Festival Hall where the programme included her favourite composers, Vivaldi and Mozart. From Vivaldi they played Concertos 5 and 12 and part of *Il cimento dell'armonia e dell'invencione,* that she liked much more than the better-known first four concertos. And from Mozart, the "Concerto for Piano Number Nine", whose third movement, inevitably, reminded her of the laughter and games of her small brothers and sisters as well as her own childhood pranks.

She strolled in Hyde Park, ate in a Chinese restaurant in Soho and on Sunday saw a film by Tarkovsky. At night, back in her hotel, moved by the exciting weekend, she collapsed into bed, exhausted but happy. Before falling asleep, the image of Marwan – who she remembered had changed into something unrecognisable, shut up in a psychiatric hospital – came into her mind, affecting her state of mind and her tiredness a little.

The next night she caught a bus to Paris. It was the cheapest way of making the journey. When she arrived at seven o'clock in the morning at *Place Stalingrad Station*, she felt worn out but happy. She waited until half past eight to telephone Philippe, the fellow student she had met at the congress, to ask him to come and collect her. He arrived within a few minutes in a Renault. During the journey, Helena was amazed by the beauty of Paris and by the crazy way in which the Parisians drove, as bad as, or perhaps worse than, the drivers in Mexico City. It was so far removed from the courtesy of British drivers. She noted that, whereas practically all the cities that she knew had a certain number of special places of interest or sights, Paris, the whole city itself, is one great sight. There was no need to wait to see the "places of tourist interest" because all of Paris is just that: every street and alley, including the boulevards that Haussmann walked along – which is, in fact, everything.

Philippe's parents lived in the 6th Arrondissement, in a small street between *Place d'Iéna* and the *Arc de Triomphe*. It was on the top two floors of a building inhabited by the upper middle class. Philippe's room was on the top floor; it had a balcony with a fine view in the direction of the *Arc de Triomphe* and much of Paris.

Philippe's father was a shareholder in a prominent medical research company which was known world-wide.

After meeting Philippe's parents at breakfast, Helena set out for the University of Paris to meet Professor Bergé, with whom she had an appointment. Once she had left Philippe's house, she felt more relaxed because she was free from having to tolerate the pseudo-aristocratic atmosphere and arrogance of those who didn't cease to refer to her as "Philippe's little Mexican girlfriend". Their references to Mexico and Latin America merely demonstrated their enormous ignorance and prejudices, like when, on showing her to her room, Philippe's mother asked her, with her exquisite manners, if she had been vaccinated against cholera and malaria.

Her conversation with Professor Bergé, who was so interested and friendly, reminded her of her first meetings with Professor Jackson at Cambridge. They visited the laboratories, and during the afternoon she gave a talk which was attended by numerous research students and undergraduates. They were all members of the Institute, where they discussed, in great detail, the experimental techniques and the results which she had obtained. In the evening, she was accompanied by several students to the *Quartier Latin* where, in a small restaurant, they ate *crêpes* washed down with a bottle of *Beaujolais*.

Very early the next morning, accompanied by Lin, an extremely nice young student of Vietnamese origin whom she had met the previous day at the Institute, she visited the Louvre where they both spent almost the whole day under a kind of magic spell admiring the artistic treasures contained there. Although they felt it was irrational, they were amused by the fact that Lin knew as little about the culture of Latin America, past or present, as Helena knew about Oriental civilisation. They identified with each other and found a common language as soon as they spoke about theatre, painting, sculpture, music or European literature and, to fill in their gaps, decided to talk about their cultural roots.

Later, intrigued, Lin asked her why she was staying with Philippe.

"Well, because I don't have to pay a hotel bill, and because when we were in London he was kind enough to invite me. Why do you ask?"

"Philippe and his family are known to be militant members of the French National Front Party and, to be frank, it seems strange to me that, as you are Mexican, he has invited you. Perhaps because of your chestnut hair and white skin people don't think of you as typically Mexican and so he invited you without knowing where you were from."

"Now I know why they are so keen on exploring the European roots of my family tree…"

In the evening, she found out that Laurette, Philippe's sister, was having a party at home on the terrace. At the invitation of her host, Helena attended. The view of Paris and the *Arc de Triomphe* by night was fabulous, as was the drink, *Moët et Chandon* champagne, and the canapés of red and black caviar and *foie gras* served in a variety of ways.

After one drink, they left the terrace and went inside to dance a little, but the volume and intensity of the music made Helena go back outside. Some guests joined in Philippe and Helena's conversation which quickly degenerated into jokes of a racist nature. Excusing herself by saying that she had already had quite a lot to drink and that she was tired, Helena said goodnight and went down to her room. Once she was alone, since she was neither tired nor inebriated, she wandered through the elegant drawing-room where a fine mahogany bookcase was resplendent with its collection of richly bound books. Glancing casually at some of the titles, she read, *The Thousand Best Cooking Recipes, Encyclopaedia of Paranormal Phenomena, My Struggle,…* With this range of titles she couldn't help remembering her visit in Mexico, to a house belonging to a family similar to Philippe's, not only because of their aristocratic pretensions, but because in their elegant drawing-room there had also been a beautiful mahogany bookcase with books carefully bound in leather, where she had found one entitled *Stories*; when she had taken it out and opened it, expecting to find something by Maupassant, Chekhov or Wilde, she had found some short stories by Walt Disney. Helena was thinking about this when Philippe, obviously drunk, came into the drawing-room. Staggering about, he made straight for her and violently grabbed her by the waist, pressing his mouth on her neck. During the struggle they fell into an armchair.

"Laisse-moi!"

"Putaine mexicaine de merde!"

After hitting him a couple of times, Helena managed to get free, and with her blouse torn she fled to her room and locked herself in.

The following morning Helena had breakfast with Philippe's parents. She thanked them for their hospitality and said goodbye. The rest of the day she spent strolling around Paris. She bought some books. She decided to take the train back to London rather than the coach. It was more expensive, but she was very tired. She booked a couchette and travelled at night in comfort. During the journey she re-read Victor Hugo's *Quatre-vingt-treize*, which she had dipped into when she was an adolescent and which now she had been unable to resist buying when she had chanced upon it in a bookshop.

Back in London she felt happy and thought that, although it wasn't as splendid as Paris, it was, however, filled with an exquisite charm. She was fascinated by its districts with identical houses, one after another, its gloomy streets, but above all by its open spaces, which in Paris were all too conspicuous by their absence. She immediately caught a train to Cambridge and arrived shortly after midday. She left her case in her flat and made her way to the dining-room of the Institute as she had not had any breakfast and was very hungry. After choosing her food at the counter of the self-service restaurant, she picked up her tray and looked around for a table. She saw one where some Iraqi and English students were talking in loud voices. She didn't like any of them much, but with the object of hearing something about Marwan she sat down with them.

"How are things? How is Marwan? It's almost a fortnight now since I have heard anything about him," said Helena in a friendly way as she prepared to eat.

"That's who we're talking about. Poor bloke, he's lost a screw," said one of them, whilst the others let out a chorus of laughter.

One of them began the story.

"We've been going to the hospital ever since he became ill, but they wouldn't let us see him for several days; finally, when he seemed to be better, the doctor asked us to take him out for a stroll, believing it would do him good. We took him to McDonald's. Marwan suddenly got up and went to the toilet; when he returned we carried on eating and chatting until four policemen arrived who barred the entrance to the restaurant. When the policemen came in, Marwan got up and ran towards them, shouting and pointing at us, 'It's them; they're the ones who want to kill me!' The police arrested us and questioned us. Later we found out that Marwan had written a message on the mirror in the toilet which read, 'Quick, call the police, because they want to kill me.' The police officers realised that Marwan was crazy, and they took him back to the psychiatric hospital."

Helena listened to this story with dismay and stopped eating, whilst the others around the table couldn't contain their mirth.

"Is Marwan in hospital?" she asked.

"No, the day before yesterday he was sent back to Iraq; he's completely mad."

Without saying a word Helena got up from the table and left the restaurant. She rang the hospital and confirmed that Marwan was no longer there. She felt a lump in her throat that scarcely allowed her to breathe. She went out for a walk in the park and wept floods of tears. She remembered Marwan's friendly and impartial manner and also his advice and help, thanks to which she had been able to forge ahead with her own research. She remembered him as tall and frail, with his black hair and his large sunken eyes which always had the look of a timid child. She went on weeping until it began to get dark and she decided to go back to her flat. Still sobbing, she tried to sleep.

Over the next few days she spent little time in the laboratory; she tried to get home early, to be alone. It was during this time that she had the opportunity to get to know something about the daily life of her flatmates, Nancy and James. She came to truly admire James' powers of concentration but to abhor Nancy's complete lack of consideration for others.

Every day after lunch, Nancy would get back to the flat and, as a musical background to whatever she was doing – be it sleeping, reading or writing letters – she would switch on her stereo and have the music blaring out at full blast as if in a dance hall – at least, that's how it seemed to Helena – until between seven and nine at night when she would go out to the cinema or to a pub with her friends. James, who usually worked on his mathematical problems lying back in an armchair, was indifferent to whether Nancy had her music on or not, which Helena found surprising. He would be completely cut off from the outside world, studying until ten o'clock at night; then he would go off to some pub or other to have a beer. She truly admired his self-discipline and powers of concentration. Because of James's attitude and, without doubt, also owing to Nancy's intolerable music, Helena decided to go back to her customary work routine, spending a minimum of twelve hours in the laboratory.

The memory of Marwan haunted her but she felt powerless. She had to accept the situation and continue working efficiently. By now, with the experience she had acquired during the recent congress, she was able to sketch clearly the direction in which her research should go. She realised that her results were fairly good and also what she should do to complement them when presenting her doctoral thesis.

She also decided not to go into the Institute dining-room in order to avoid meeting the Iraqi students and Peter, her work-bench companion.

Whilst having a meal in the restaurant of a nearby college, she noted that a bearded youth seated opposite her was reading a book in Spanish: *Poesia* by J. L. Borges. Enthused, she interrupted him asking,
"Where are you from? Do you like Borges?"

"I'm Greek, and of course I like Borges, although I lack the necessary words to express adequately how much I like him." His accent was almost perfect. What about you? Where are you from and what are you doing here?"

"I'm Mexican and I'm studying biology."

"Ah, Mexican!... Like Borges, you've been sent to Europe to complete your education and to broaden your outlook. Isn't that right?"

"Yes, although it's interesting that you can count on the fingers of one hand the number of Europeans who leave their continent to complete their education and broaden their outlook."

"The point is that, as Borges had already noted, in Europe there are no Europeans. There are Frenchmen, Englishmen, Germans, Greeks, etc., etc., but there are no Europeans."

"And he was absolutely right," laughed Helena.

"It's ridiculous that this continent, which has given so many universal human values to the world should be, at the same time, so provincial. What's your name?"

"Helena. And yours?"

"Andrópulos, and, in anticipation of your next question, I'm about to complete my doctorate in philosophy."

"What philosophical problem have you been working on?"

"Firstly, we should establish what we mean by the term 'philosophical problem', as it is a concept that has evolved quite a bit. Traditionally, many of the 'philosophical problems' dealt with questions related to the origins or destiny of mankind and of the universe. However, it is difficult nowadays to find a philosopher vain enough to try to answer these questions, or who dreams of defining how one should lead one's life. These days, since Russell, Moore and Wittgenstein, we try to be more modest, and we have abandoned the universe to students of natural sciences, limiting philosophy to research into the rules of language, the passport to human knowledge. Ancient 'philosophical problems' constitute an expression which is the product of an inadequate use of language. That means that we see philosophy as the study of language and not as the means of responding to the great questions about life and the universe."

"How come you speak Spanish so well?"

"I started studying it on my own, in order to read *Quijote*, and after finishing my degree in Greece I worked as a correspondent in Central America for various news agencies."

"And you read *Quijote*?"

"When I tried at first I couldn't. It's written in very difficult Spanish. Perhaps now I could do it."

"Which Latin American countries have you been to?"

"Mainly Nicaragua, El Salvador, Honduras and Costa Rica, although I have also spent a short time in Argentina."

"I envy you! There are two things which bind me inseparably to Argentina: Borges and the tango."

"The tango? You like the tango? But in Mexico you have your *mariachis*, said Andrópulos, pronouncing the word with difficulty.

"The words of most tangos and *mariachi* songs are rubbish; they speak of prostitutes, machos, and extra-marital affairs. However, the music and the rhythm of the tango seem to me to be infinitely richer than the music of *mariachis*."

"Without doubt, you're an exceptional Mexican," said Andrópulos, smiling.

Helena was surprised by the ease with which this conversation developed, and thought that it must have been because of an intense and mutual personal empathy as well as the boredom and depression that she had been feeling. From this first meeting onwards they continued to meet at weekends, to cook their national dishes and savour them. Helena had never tasted a more exquisite moussaka, always accompanied by ouzo as an aperitif and then Greek wine.

"The boring thing is to have to cook every day," commented Andrópulos, "but doing it now and then is very pleasant. Cooking is a very creative activity, similar, I think, to what a painter, composer or novelist does; the difference is that it doesn't last. I find it very relaxing as well."

For her part, Helena did her best to prepare stuffed chillies, *guacamole*, fried kidney beans, as well as some stews she had invented, such as: "Meat with mushrooms a la Guanajuato", and some others which were produced out of the mere desire to experiment. In time she came to share the same opinion of cooking as Andrópulos. Besides, such moments were an opportunity to calmly finish off some of their innumerable conversations that they had had in the college restaurant and were never able to finish because of lack of time.

"Just think," said Helena, "only a week ago, Nancy, my flatmate, was hysterical because on the M.A. literature programme she is following, an elective course is required. This year the only choice they offered was Latin American literature, and in particular, the works of Alejo Carpentier. Have you read him?"

"Of course I have! He's the Victor Hugo of Latin America!"

"That's a good way of describing him... I, too, think that he could only be compared with writers of the stature of Hugo."

"Right. And why did Nancy get hysterical?"

"Because she knows nothing about the subject and, moreover, she's not interested."

"How can that be?"

"I think she is a little snob who is only interested in holidays and in not complicating her life. She spends her time reading huge quantities of 'literature' which is nothing but rubbish. On one occasion when I saw her finish a novel, I tried to get her to comment on what she had read, but she did nothing but talk about frivolous stories of sex and romance with no serious content. I asked her to lend me the book, and after I had read it I realised it wasn't possible to make any comment about such stuff."

"I would take that as an excuse to speculate. I have often asked myself how it is possible to know how to evaluate a literary text."

"Yes, I have also thought about what criteria you might apply to say that something is very good or very bad. For example, you could judge a novel by the richness of its language, and in this case writers like James Joyce or Alejo Carpentier would be excellent models. But you could also consider the skill with which the plot is woven, and we should have Edgar Allan Poe as one of the great masters. Marcel Proust would be the winner if we were considering the writer's descriptive ability."

"Oh, yes, Proust, that intolerable fellow: the reader has gone but he carries on talking. He's definitely got verbal diarrhoea. To describe what a character feels or sees in a flash can take him up to five pages of incredibly dense prose. Of course the opposite also exists, like the present-day writer: the poor fellow has no sooner described one action than he's onto the next."

"On the other hand, the criterion for judgement could be the historical authenticity of the subject or the collection of subjects, and here again Carpentier would occupy a very special place alongside others, such as Leo Tolstoy."

"And Plato! That inspired writer whom we must thank for inventing Socrates, that most fascinating of literary characters. Yes, I see the drift in your argument; we could carry on by saying that if the criterion is entertainment, then writers like John Kennedy Toole or Chesterton are masters, don't you agree?"

Andrópulos helped himself to a little more wine and said that it would be better to search for a universal criterion for judging literature.

"I think you are right, but if you knew the things that Nancy read, I am sure that you would agree with me that it was rubbish. What I want to know is, strictly speaking, what criterion are we to apply in order to say that it's rubbish? What concerns me is that at any moment a stupid critic may come along, as happens all too often, who analyses this dustbin literature using 'in-depth analysis' and comes to the conclusion that it is a 'work of genius', citing the 'incredible way in which the inner world of the characters is presented', 'the use of style without style' or 'the unique structure of the plot'. What I am saying does not sound so ridiculous when we already know that two of the greatest writers of this century, Carpentier and Borges, were not awarded the Nobel prize for literature, whilst others, virtually unknown, were. Fortunately, to their credit, some of them expressed great surprise because, in their opinion, other writers deserved it more than they did."

"I agree with you, but you cannot ignore the serious political interests that influence the awarding of the Nobel prizes. They could hardly have handed the prize over to Carpentier because he was Cuban and a committed supporter of Fidel Castro. To have awarded him the prize would have been interpreted as recognition of the success of certain aspects of the Cuban Revolution, and that is something few people would accept. But, to return to the original question, I think that we should judge a literary text by its universality and the poetic way in which this is expressed."

"Frankly, although we agree which texts are or are not rubbish, it would be impossible for anyone to lay down infallible 'rules' to settle the question. I am concerned to find so many young people like Nancy who consume this 'literature' and base their criteria for judgement upon it."

"That worries me, too, but I think there are a number of reasons for it. One is that the rest of the world has not seen a literary explosion as spectacular as that of Latin America. Start making a list and you immediately have writers like: Borges, Carpentier, Cortázar, García Márquez, Alfonso Reyes, Vargas Llosa, Carlos Fuentes, Juan Carlos Onetti, Roa Bastos, Uslar Pietri, José Donoso, Octavio Paz, Neruda, Rulfo, etc., etc." (Each time he said "etcetera", Andrópulos raised his hand.) "Moreover, these are writers who experienced, or who are experiencing, very complex social and political problems, and what is important is that young Latin American readers also continue to experience similar problems. In Europe, meanwhile, what is happening? Young readers of today have nothing in common with the great European writers and the historical problems which confronted them. For them everything is resolved; they live so well that all that matters to them is to read novels like the ones Nancy reads, and not to have to face up to, because they do not need to, the social problems and intellectual balancing acts now so typical of Latin Americans."

"I am amazed that you, as a European, should think like that."

"Well, it's one thing to be Greek and another not to see what is happening here, although it is still a matter of regret that this is taking place in Europe, the cultural cradle of the Western World."

"In time all cradles end up smelling of piss, as Alejo Carpentier is supposed to have said."

"And I think he's absolutely right," laughed Andrópulos. "Look, let me read you one of the most marvellous passages I have ever read."

He picked up a book and, switching from English to Spanish, read:

Gracias quiero dar al divino

laberinto de los efectos y de las causas

por la diversidad de las criaturas

que forman este singular universo,

"You see what a wonderful way of speaking about God, if He does in fact exist, without mentioning His name?"

por la razon, que no cesará de sonar

con un plano del laberito,

"I cannot imagine a more beautiful way of expressing the innate desire of mankind to understand the universe which surrounds him."

Andrópulos continued:

por el amor, que nos deja ver a los otros

como los ve la divinidad,

"Anyone who has ever been in love knows how true this is!" cried Andrópulos. "And what is so wonderful is the almost magic way of talking about the everyday world, the universe, the epistemological problem that this represents, love... By the way, have you ever been in love?"

"When I was much younger. What about you?"

"I am in love now. I love a girl from Honduras, and I assure you that Borges is right: if a divine being exists he would be able to see us only as I see my girlfriend.

"Well, listen to this:

por el fulgor del fuego

que ningún ser humano puede mirar sin un asombro antiguo,

por el arte de la amistad,

por el último día de Sócrates,

por el lenguaje, que puede simular la sabiduría,

"That last verse is so majestic!" exclaimed Helena. "Wittgenstein would have loved it."

por la mañana, que nos depara la ilusión de un principio,

por los íntimos dones que no enumero,

por la música, misteriosa forma del tiempo.

The next time they met, Andrópulos spoke even more romantically about Cristina, his girlfriend from Honduras. Helena asked him if he had thought about living in Honduras or Europe.

"What I would like to do is to live in Latin America; that is the greatest challenge. There, everything, or almost everything, has yet to be done, although I realise that it would be easier to be based in Europe."

Helena was pleased to hear him speak so enthusiastically of Cristina, above all because, as she commented, in Mexico it is rare for a man to have the confidence to speak to a woman in that way. Machismo seldom allows a genuine friendship between a man and a woman to develop without a sexual dimension.

"You should not idealise things. In Europe, the form that machismo takes is no different from that in Latin America. What is more, in my opinion, in an urban environment, in Europe or Latin America, the likelihood of encountering a male chauvinist or a submissive woman – the basic requirement for the existence of the chauvinist – is just about the same."

"If what you say is true then perhaps I have been a little foolish."

"Why?"

"Because I found chauvinism so unpleasant, I rejected nearly all the male friends I had in Mexico."

*****

On one particular occasion, Andrópulos arrived at Helena's laboratory unexpectedly, as they had already had lunch together.

"You wouldn't believe it, but just after you left I met two very nice Mexicans, René and Roberto. They invited me to a party they're having this evening and asked me to bring a lady friend along. Would you like to come with me?"

"I'd love to!" said Helena, who was by then feeling rather tired of preparing samples for her experiments.

When they arrived they were welcomed by René and Roberto.

"Hello! You're really early! It is only seven o'clock and we said nine."

"I'm so sorry," said Andrópulos, "I misunderstood. If you like, we can come back later or, better still, help with the preparations."

"O.K. Come in."

"Let me introduce you to Helena, who is also Mexican."

"Hello."

They were surprised how big the house was. It had two storeys and an enormous garden. They couldn't help noticing a BMW and a Jaguar in the large garage.

"How can you pay for all this?" asked Helena a bit flustered.

"We have an income in addition to the grant we get from CONACYT. Our families also help out," said René, pouring some whiskey and soda.

"What do you do?" asked Andrópulos.

"I work for PEMEX, the national petroleum company," said Roberto, "and René is an adviser with the federal government."

"Well, you are not working at the moment. Are you having a year off?" asked Andrópulos.

"No, it is simply that we have *friends.*"

"We are *consultants,*" interrupted René with a laugh.

"What do you mean by saying you're *consultants* and have *friends*?"

"Having *friends* means having good political contacts and being *consultants* means that thanks to our *friends* we do not have to be physically present at work," explained René, gulping down a large whisky and smoothing down his hair rather compulsively."

"Come on, tell me more," said Andrópulos, very interested.

"Look," said René, "my father is a deputy in the PRI."

"What's the PRI?"

"It's the Partido Revolucionario Institucional (Institutional Revolutionary Party) and it's been in power under one name or another ever since the Mexican Revolution," replied Helena.

"Exactly," agreed René, carrying on talking at the top of his voice. "That's how my father managed to get me this job as a consultant with the federal government, which gives me an income to top up my grant from CONACYT."

"As for me," interrupted Roberto, "my father works for the national union of PEMEX, and that's how I got my job."

"But it's not really above board, is it?" asked Andrópulos.

"In Mexico there are worse things going on than that and, as we say at home, if money is being thrown away on things that don't help us, then it may as well come our way," said René.

Roberto interrupted him and carried on in a strong accent that Helena recognised as typical of Mexico City. "Mexico is a country of great social contrasts and the government frequently wants to help the people, but the truth is that the people are very ignorant. For example, they spend millions in subsidies and on economic aid to the peasants, and it's of absolutely no use to them because they are stupid, dumb, foolish. Do you understand? And they are also very lazy."

"What are you studying?"

"When I qualified as an accountant I wanted to travel around the world, so I decided it would be a good idea to take advantage of my father's connection with CONACYT and ask for a grant to come here to do a master's degree," said René. "Besides, my fiancée's in Mexico; we want to get married, and I've already got a job lined up for when I get back."

"As what? You said you were a consultant, didn't you?"

"Oh, that's only whilst I am here in England; I shall become mayor of a provincial town when I get back to Mexico; it's a small town but I have to start my political career somewhere," said René, swiftly changing the cassette on the stereo. They went on talking and drinking.

"What about you, Helena, what are you studying?" asked Roberto.

"Biology," replied Helena brusquely, as she was beginning to feel rather uncomfortable with the conversation. She thought it was going to be very difficult to conceal her profound dislike of René and Roberto.

"When you arrived I thought you were more than just friends," said Roberto.

"No, just friends," explained Andrópulos.

"Didn't you have problems getting your parents to let you come here to England alone?" asked René.

"No, my parents had long known that I wanted to study for my doctorate abroad, so it was no surprise to them."

"Mine wouldn't have let my sisters go off alone, and I must say I agree with them, as a woman needs more of an eye kept on her so that she doesn't go astray," expressed René.

"What do you mean, 'go astray'?" interrupted Helena.

"Well, for example, have an affair with a man who has gone astray."

"That's rubbish; a woman has just as much right to do what she likes in her sexual life as a man does."

"You're a Christian, aren't you?" asked René.

"I'm tired of this nonsense. Juárez has already said, and quite rightly, that what people need is a religion that obliges them to read rather than buy candles."

"Incidentally," Roberto butted in, pouring more whisky and passing out the snacks that he was making, "something odd happened to me with an Irish girl. I chatted with her all night, and then we began kissing and caressing, but when we were naked and aroused, what do think she said to me? That she wasn't going to have sex because she was a Christian. It's unbelievable! Don't you agree? In Mexico I have come across girls who didn't want to have sex because they were menstruating, or because they didn't fancy me, or because they didn't feel like it, but no woman has ever told me that she wouldn't have sex because she was a Christian."

"Of course," interrupted Helena, "although more than ninety per cent of Mexicans say they are Christian, Christianity in Mexico is pure fiesta and folklore; they love pilgrimages, the *posadas* and generally having a good time. Religious precepts don't matter one iota to them. Here I have met very few religious people, but those who are, whether Muslim, Hindu, Anglican or whatever, before carrying out any act whatsoever, however ordinary it may be, consider it and analyse it in accordance with their religious principles; whereas in Mexico, people say they really are Catholic, and they beat their breasts a lot, but they rob, lie and even kill as a matter of routine, without it troubling their conscience at all."

At that moment the doorbell rang and René and Roberto got up to go into the garden to welcome the guests who had just arrived. Meanwhile, Helena said to Andrópulos, "These people represent the Mexico that I hate the most – the one full of cynics, sycophants, the corrupt and the self-righteous. Let's go when you have finished your drink."

"Right. In fact, I realised from the expression on your face during the conversation that you didn't like them very much."

Two Germans and three English girls came into the house – the girls already a little worse for drink – and they all introduced themselves. Out of necessity, the conversation went from Spanish into English, and Helena noted that René and Roberto spoke very little English.

The Germans dominated the conversation at first, talking about their last visit to the Canaries, and then René called Helena into the kitchen and, using a tone of voice that was over-paternalistic, said, "Helena, I am concerned about some of the comments you made when we were chatting and, with the best of intentions, I should like to give you this book which was a present to me from my father and which, in the most difficult moments of my life, has helped me enormously."

Helena found herself looking at a book entitled, *Gotas de amor, reflexiones sobre la vida de Cristo*[1], astonished at what René was saying to her. "It's a book that will help you to not make mistakes along the difficult path of life, whether the problems are big or small, or whether it's just some comfort that you need. For example, when I feel sad thinking about my fiancée, reflecting on the life and love of Christ gives me the strength to carry on fighting. It really is a special book for me, and I would like to give it to you to help you find the path of God."

Helena resisted the temptation to laugh as she was afraid of offending him, and just said, "René, I really am grateful for your interest and concern for me, but I cannot accept your gift basically because I don't believe in any religion, and I don't consider believing to be a necessary condition for leading a moral life. Moreover, I don't think it's right that if your father gave you this book, thinking about you and your spiritual well-being, you should now be giving it to me, but thank you, anyway."

She left him and went into the lounge where she saw there were several guests. She sat next to Andrópulos who was listening to Roberto chatting with Hans, one of the German guests.

"So you have been to Mexico. Good for you! I'm going to put on some Mexican music." Roberto got up from the group and put on a cassette of *mariachi* music; he also opened a bottle of tequila, sat down again and asked as he served the drinks, "And what did you think of Mexico? What places did you visit?"

---

[1]*Drops of Love: Reflections on the Life of Christ*

"I was in the centre and south-east of the country. I liked it very much. The archaeological remains are rather impressive; the people are very warm; the vegetation is so beautiful, and the beaches are fabulous."

They went on chatting about Hans's visit to Mexico, encouraged by Roberto who continued serving tequila. Meanwhile, others were dancing or trying to dance to the Mexican music which was being played at full blast. Helena got up, indicating to Andrópulos that she was just going to the bathroom and then they could leave. They told her that the bathroom was on the top floor. She went upstairs into a small room with three identical doors. She opened one of them at random and saw two nude bodies making love on a bed: it was René and one of the English girls. She quickly shut the door and laughingly muttered to herself, "You should get her to read your father's book."

When she got back to the lounge she noticed Hans and Roberto talking animatedly. She decided to sit down by Andrópulos who seemed very amused.

"The real problem is the tremendous poverty there is everywhere in Mexico," said Hans. "You eat in a very exclusive restaurant, and as you leave you find beggars, women and children sleeping in the street."

"We all see what we want to see," retorted Roberto, angrily. "There is poverty just as there is all over the world, but they also live very well, perhaps better than in Europe. I came here thinking I would find a high standard of living, and there are only medium-sized houses or flats comparable to those of the Mexican middle class. The one I have in Mexico is eight hundred square metres, without counting the gardens; we have five cars and have at least one holiday a year in the United States or Canada, as well as the trips that my father and his friends make in the company plane to Las Vegas to play cards or roulette. How many Europeans live like that? The truth is that we are better off than you."

"I've no doubt that there are some Mexicans who live like you. However, I prefer to live here, where practically everybody has all that they need, than in a country with a corrupt government, where the élite live like kings and the bulk of the population lives in poverty or on the edge of it."

"That's slanderous; corruption is the same whether here or in Mexico – or anywhere in the world."

Helena, who had become interested in the conversation, decided to interrupt. "You have to distinguish between large-scale and small-scale corruption. I think that the cases of major corruption, involving the highest economic and political circles, possibly occur just as frequently in Mexico as in Europe. But the cases of small-scale corruption, like the typical bribe that in Mexico you give to a traffic policeman or to a bureaucrat in a government office, occur more frequently there than in Europe because of the starvation wages that many workers receive. It's the only way they can supplement their income. Don't take this to mean that I am justifying small-scale corruption, I am merely trying to explain why it exists in Mexico but generally not in Europe."

"Besides, in Europe, if they catch someone mixed up in a case of small- or large-scale corruption, it is absolutely certain that they are not going to get off lightly, but I am not sure if that would be the case in Mexico. What's the matter, for example, with political corruption and democracy in Mexico?" asked Hans.

"Mexico is a democratic country with free elections just like any European country," snapped Roberto.

Helena added with a laugh, "How can Mexico be a democratic country when a few hours ago, before everyone arrived, you told us about how you spent your summer holidays 'working' at PEMEX, playing cards inside huge empty storage barrels? And then you told us that you had to pay for obtaining your twenty-eight day contract by supporting the PRI demonstrations. And how a worker, who didn't become a member of PRI and didn't vote for it, was automatically dismissed from his job. And how, before each election, your father made you, when you were a small boy, fill whole boxes with ballot papers 'voting' for the PRI. I think it would be more honest to accept the evidence and recognise that Mexico is a country with a party dictatorship, that it is a stranger to democracy, and where inequality, violence and political crime are common practice."

"You are unpatriotic," interrupted Roberto furiously, "and you obviously want the renegades of PAN or the Communists to be in power."

"All I want is for the people to be respected. The PRI has no reason to be Mexico's police force. I remember when I was eight years old and a PRI presidential candidate visited my town. By the instructions of the mayor of the town, all the children in the state schools were taken out to welcome him. Seven hours standing out in the sun! Many children fainted and became dehydrated. At last, in a flash, the presidential candidate went past in his bus, and we were ordered to clap and cheer. When I got home I felt used and humiliated. I can assure you that the seed of indignation has been growing ever since."

"Look, Roberto, don't take it as a personal insult," said Hans, trying to calm things down. "In all frankness, I can tell you that when I was in Mexico, I saw that many people, in particular the indigenous people and the peasants, lived in houses a thousand times worse than the cowsheds occupied by European cattle."

"Those people live like that because it's part of their culture," shouted Roberto, obviously very put out. "We don't need stupid German tourists to come and tell us about it."

"Part of their culture? Then, according to that argument, as my ancestors lived in caves for centuries, you could justify their continuing to do so. I assure you that no compatriot of mine would swap his centrally-heated house and his Mercedes for a cave... This 'cultural' argument seems rather the justification invented by a corrupt and inept government, incapable of raising the standard of living of its people."

Roberto jumped on Hans and they started fighting. Andrópulos and Helena got up and ran out of the house, jumped on their bicycles and rode away, with the noise of objects being smashed, shouts and *mariachi* music gradually growing fainter.

"Do you know what?" said Helena. "These Mexicans remind me of the stereotype drawn by Alan Riding: the Mexicans who by themselves destroy their country with their comments and reveal with complete cynicism its corruption and rottenness, but as soon as there are foreigners present, become ridiculously fanatical patriots – they are unbearable."

"I learnt a lot tonight and I really enjoyed myself."

Switching to other matters, Helena, doubling up with laughter, told him about René's attempts to moralise.

They found out later that Roberto had given up his studies and returned to Mexico and that René, who because of some administrative error by CONACYT had received fifteen thousand dollars one month instead of the usual thousand, had also left Cambridge and set off to "go round the world" before returning to Mexico.

One day, when they were eating in the college restaurant, Andrópulos said to Helena, "We have known each other for over a year, and I have noticed that you don't use diminutives as frequently as most Mexicans who are always talking about 'little moments', 'little glasses', etcetera. Why not?"

"It must be because when I was a small girl my father never allowed us to use them, and every time we asked for a '*little* glass of a *little* drop of milk', or something like that, he would say in a deep, loud, vibrating voice that made us tremble, 'It's not a *little* glass or a *little* drop of milk.' My parents had some friends called Margarita and Agapito and I ended up calling them Márgara and Agapo," she said with a smile. "Look, I want to read you this passage – I'd really like to know what you think of it. Listen:

42

Elena tocó la puerta y habló en su medio italiano y puso los higos frescos sobre la mesa y dijo que el día estaba muy hermoso y guiñó un ojo. Javier se levantó de la cama y Elena rió gritando y mostró sus dientes picados y miró a Javier entre los dedos muy separados que cubrían su rostro y se santiguó entre carcajadas y dijo que el mundo sería mejor si el señor pudiera mostrarse así en la playa...

[Helena knocked on the door and spoke in her broken Italian and put the fresh figs on the table and said that it was a very beautiful day and winked. Javier got out of bed and Helena shrieked with laughter and showed her sharp teeth and looked at Javier between her outstretched fingers which were covering her face and crossed herself between bursts of laughter and said that the world would be a better place if the gentleman could show himself on the beach in that way..."]

"It's a little hard on the ear." said Andrópulos. "There are too many 'ands'."

"I agree. You will be interested to know that it was written by Carlos Fuentes, indisputably one of the most talented of Latin American writers. I wonder what would have happened if it had been written by me or some other unknown writer."

"Well, it would have been rejected by the publishers."

"Yes, and perhaps with a letter of rejection that stressed the need to take a basic course in writing," she laughed as she carved an unappetising slice of roast beef. "It's important to realise that if it had been written by someone unknown, they would have said, 'It's the work of a beginner,' 'it contains glaring errors,' whereas if it had been written by someone well known, they would have said, 'It's so eloquent.' 'It shows such command of the language.' 'How original!'"

"Would you prefer a work to stand on its own merit, regardless of who had written it?"

"Well," replied Helena, "the *Iliad, Beowulf* and many other works rely on their own merit, independent of their authors."

"That reminds me of something I have just read by Umberto Eco. Let's suppose that a student has written a doctoral thesis about contemporary Latin American literature. It would be considered a serious mistake if he had not included certain writers; however, if a work on the same theme were written by a writer or critic already well known and did not include certain authors, any reader would know that it was not owing to an error. He is clearly expressing his opinion by not mentioning them. Therefore, in the final analysis it does matter who the writer is."

"That could well be so in certain cases. I think that any work of literature, if that's what it really is, must exist beyond its author and what he intends." She took a large sip of lemonade and continued, "You know, I also want to tell you something that makes me very happy. Do you remember that I told you that I hadn't received my grant from CONACYT for several months? Well, to start with I lived off my savings, but for two months I have been spending weekends writing essays on Latin American literature and writers for students of literature who pay me thirty pounds for each one ..."

"Helena, if you need money I can lend you some with the greatest of pleasure."

"I have sent several telegrams to Mexico to let them know I had not received my grant, and they have assured me that the following month it would all be sorted out. What I'm really pleased about is that I have been told the marks that I have received for my work, and they are quite acceptable. At first I was concerned whether what I was doing was ethical, but finally I concluded that if they have to apportion blame, let them blame life."

"Deep down, doesn't it make you feel sad?"

"More than sad, betrayed. Apart from rare exceptions like you, almost all young Europeans I have met – whether university students or not – are incredibly ignorant and apathetic. In Mexico I had friends who were studying civil engineering, anthropology, mathematics, etcetera, and – although not one of us was a 'doctor' of political science, human or exact – we were tremendously interested in any subject and just as likely to talk about the theory of relativity, the cinema or Renaissance painting as the political situation in Vietnam or Angola. That doesn't happen here. What is serious is that even young people who are supposed to be deeply involved in a particular discipline, like Nancy and her fellow students of literature, display incredible apathy towards subjects to do with their own speciality.

*****

A few months later Andrópulos completed his thesis and obtained his doctorate. Helena sadly bade him farewell at the airport upon his return to Thessalonika. They were taken aback by the mutual feeling that came over them, despite Andrópulos' happiness at having obtained his doctorate and at the prospect of soon being reunited with Cristina. As they said goodbye they both felt a lump in their throats which only a long – and perhaps also yearned for – kiss could relieve.

Nancy obtained her M.A. with a thesis and two final essays; one of these was on *La consagracion de la primavera*[2] by Alejo Carpentier, which Helena had greatly enjoyed writing. Nancy was happy to have been awarded her M.A. and decided to travel a little before returning to the United States. She bought a package holiday to Tel Aviv and Cairo, which she almost immediately sold to Helena at half price, as she had to return unexpectedly to the United States for her sister's wedding.

Helena was pleasantly surprised to find herself on board an El Al plane bound for Tel Aviv. She had never before thought of making such a trip and was pleased to be able to take a week's break from her

---

[2]*The Consecration of Spring*
(Published as *The Rite of Spring*)

strict work routine and have a short rest. She found it immensely exciting to be travelling to a country with such a controversial recent history. Moreover, the fact that Israel was one of the countries with the greatest number of scientists *per capita* and whose educational standards were amongst the highest in the world made her feel keener than ever to make the visit.

She found Tel Aviv very impressive, especially as it was just like any other modern European city. Somehow she had been expecting something different. Her visit to the National Museum of Art was one of her most pleasurable experiences. She joined one of the many groups of children visiting the museum. It wasn't monstrous like the Louvre or the British Museum, but had at least one major work representing each school, period and artistic movement.

"What colour dominates this painting?"

"What do you think the blue mark on the left represents?"

"What do you think the painter wanted to express in this painting?"

"What do you feel when you look at this painting?"

These were some of the many questions the group of children, between the ages of six and twelve, which Helena had joined, answered for the guide in the modern art gallery. "Of course! This is the way to awaken children's interest in and love of art," Helena reflected; while a little way away she saw another guide questioning a group of children on the aesthetics of matter and space, using her hands to illustrate what she was saying and a piece of sculpture that was nearby.

"Yes," the guide said to Helena, "we try to give them the best we can when they are young so that later on we can select the most brilliant. They are the only ones who will be allowed to enter the universities. The resources for research and higher education are limited and therefore reserved purely for the most able."

Her visit to the National Philharmonic to listen to the National Symphonic Orchestra of Israel was just as interesting although not without incident. During her three days in Tel Aviv there was only one concert advertised. Helena tried to get a ticket, but at the box office they told her that it was sold out. Feeling terribly disappointed, she moved away with her head bowed, but then went back, vigorously pulling her passport out of her bag.

"Look," she said, in an agitated and pleading way, "I'm a Mexican musician, and I have travelled more than fourteen thousand kilometres to listen to the National Symphonic Orchestra of Israel. Please don't deprive me of the pleasure. I'm prepared to stand in an aisle or next to a door in the concert hall; please sell me a ticket at twice, three or even four times its value... do let me in."

The ticket office staff were bemused but smiled as they listened to her request. Finally, one of them went into an office and came out with a ticket for Helena who was delighted to accept it. In the evening, she listened to a masterful interpretation of Tchaikovsky's "Violin Concerto" with Itzhak Perlman as the soloist, and Beethoven's "Seventh Symphony".

After swimming a little in the Mediterranean, sunbathing and reading *Israel* by Ben-Gurion, she visited Natanya, Jaffa, and a kibbutz. She felt greatly impressed by Israel. The next morning she was due to leave for Cairo, but for reasons which were far from clear, the travel agency cancelled the trip to Egypt. Faced with the problem of what to do she decided to go on a tour of Jerusalem, Hebron, Bethlehem and Jericho. The last three of which were in the sector occupied by Israel in Transjordan.

Her travelling companions on the coach were mainly retired Americans. During the journey from Tel Aviv to Jerusalem, her attention was drawn constantly to the fact that the European character, like that of Tel Aviv, was gradually disappearing and entering a new world. Arabic culture and identity were becoming more evident, as well as the state of military tension. She found the famous Wailing Wall in Jerusalem very unpleasant, above all because of the incredible fanaticism that was exhibited there. As she was soon able to confirm, this is the city of religious fanaticism: Christian, Muslim or Jewish, it doesn't matter which.

As for architecture, she found the small mosques much more to her liking than the synagogues or the Catholic churches. No doubt it was because of their religious precepts which prohibited them from creating representative art, that the Muslim artists managed to achieve such excellence in the creation of geometrical and abstract shapes. Also, when she saw the superb decoration of various small mosques, she could understand why, of all the arts, calligraphy was the most highly esteemed amongst the Muslims. She was captivated by these exquisite artistic manifestations of the Muslim world and felt an immense desire to be able, one day, to travel further than the many imaginary journeys made through books, to visit the Alhambra and Baghdad, only two points of what was the Muslim Empire – an empire that at the height of its splendour extended from Spain to India, surpassing even the Roman Empire in its apogee.

At Hebron, the strong military presence and the tense state of the soldiers made her feel uneasy. This was intensified by the guide's insistence upon visiting the ruins of ancient synagogues of little artistic value, instead of the small mosques which Helena liked so much. Because of the confused explanations of the guide, perhaps believed only by some ingenuous tourists, it soon became clear to her that the interest in the ruins of synagogues had more to do with morally justifying the occupation of that territory.

She broke away from the group and walked on her own for a while until a young Arab approached her and asked in English, "Where are you from?"

"I'm from Mexico. What about you?"

"I'm from Palestine. What are you doing here? You don't seem to be an Israeli or a tourist."

"I'm here almost by accident – a friend sold me a tourist ticket that she couldn't use, very cheaply. What do you do?"

"I am studying economics, although it's really in name only, as the university operates only a maximum of three to eight weeks each academic year."

"So how do you manage?"

"We hold classes in secret, although this, too, is sometimes very dangerous, as we are liable to be arrested, beaten and sent to prison for several months."

Helena felt uncomfortable as she continued to listen to the young man telling her about the cunning and sometimes dangerous methods that he and his fellow students and teachers had to employ in order to continue their university education, despite the difficulties created by the military occupation. The depth of the youth's hatred of the Israeli government was all too clear.

"In order to understand it you would have to live in this hell, to see your grandparents forced to sell the land they had inherited from their ancestors because of direct or indirect harassment cloaked in a thousand forms, like the water supply being cut off indefinitely. Or you would need, like my parents, to see your home demolished, like any other Palestinian who may be, or who is suspected to be, sympathetic to any independence movement. Even so, they would have to demolish the houses of all Palestinian Arabs because there is no one who agrees with the occupation. Or you would have to see, like me, a friend or brother die at the hands of the Israeli army. In Palestine it is impossible to find an Arab who has not been a victim, in one way or another, of harassment or humiliation by the Israelis."

"I'm sure you are right, but you cannot go on hating and destroying one another indefinitely. You have to find a political solution to your problem of living together. Equally, it must not be forgotten that the Jewish people came here after suffering the cruel process of extermination in Europe."

"Yes, but they got here only to do the same, but now with us as the victims. The problem is that all the governments in the world, to their shame, shut their eyes to the extermination of the Jews in

Europe, and are now shutting their eyes again to the Palestinian situation – using the excuse that the Jews have already had their share of suffering. But many people have suffered and many people, like us, are suffering now. Do you know how many millions of indigenous Americans were exterminated during colonisation by the English, Spanish, French and Portuguese? Was that less cruel than the extermination of the Jews in Europe? I must confess that, in my opinion, what is most serious is that the solution to the Palestinian problem requires a social democratic revolution in the entire Arab world – which doesn't appeal to many Arab monarchies and dictatorships. They are not going to risk their own political stability to achieve the creation of a Palestinian State. The enemies of Palestine are to be found not only amongst the Israelis but also in some Arab countries. In reality, we are alone and abandoned in the world."

Helena listened to this in silence as he gazed piercingly at her with his dark eyes.

"What about you? What does the Palestinian problem matter to you? You were lucky enough to be born in a country which could give you a grant to go to England to do your doctorate and then to travel, as you are doing now. Do you realise that it's only an accident of birth? I could be in your place, accompanied by these idiot tourists you have come with, and you could be here, homeless, your brother murdered, knowing that your life offers you the stark choice of taking up arms and happily killing an Israeli soldier, or of abandoning everything and fleeing your country to start a new life, whilst you can't forget that here extermination continues."

Helena did not know what to say, and as it was time to rejoin the group, she took out of her bag the copy of *Hamlet* which she had bought in Cambridge and gave it to him.

"Excuse me for saying this, but when I saw you I thought you were different and that maybe you would understand," he said, taking a small book out of his bag: *Palestinian Stories* by G. Kanafani; then, without hiding his emotion, he placed it in her hands.

Helena was overcome with emotion; with tears in her eyes she accepted the book and went off to find the coach. From then on she would not be able to see Israel through the same eyes.

On her way back to Jerusalem, oblivious to the noise of her casual travelling companions, she read with rapt attention some biographical details about Gassan Kanafani who was considered to be the most distinguished Palestinian writer: born in Arce in 1936, settled in Damascus since 1948 and, after completing his studies, worked as a teacher and a journalist, first in Syria and then in Kuwait. Later he moved to Beirut where he began publishing the noted *Magazine Al-Hadaf* in 1969. As an active member of the Arab Nationalist Movement, he recognised that a solution to the Palestine problem would be impossible without a social revolution throughout the entire Arab world. He was assassinated by an Israeli commando unit in July 1972, when a bomb that had been placed in his car exploded. He wrote five novels, five collections of short stories, two plays and two essays on Palestinian literature.

Helena was impressed by the similarity between some of the situations described by Kanafani in his short stories and the situations in Mexico. She noted this in all its dramatic crudeness in the story "Men Under the Sun", in which three Palestinian workers, motivated by the poverty in which they live, decide to stow away in the empty cistern of a tanker in order to reach Kuwait. There they hope to find work and to be able to send petrodollars back to their families to improve their desperately low standard of living. The journey of more than 1,200 kilometres across the Jordanian and Iraqi desert ends in tragedy. In order not to be discovered they are careful not to make any noise, and so they suffocate from the intense heat. With them die their hopes, their dreams, their poverty and their tragedy. She couldn't help thinking sadly of those "dry-backs" who were so similar to the "wet-backs" in her own country.

She finished reading the book in a café in Jerusalem. The next day she would be leaving for Tel Aviv. She felt a little depressed and reflected upon the enormous admiration that Israel had initially awoken in her. At that moment, a man who had been watching her from another table came over and asked if he could join her for a while. Once he had found out that she was Mexican and how she came to be there, he asked her, "What do you think of the Arabs?"

Helena was taken aback by such a broad question and replied, "Well, they're just like any other people. Of course, like any culture, they have their own characteristics and historical development which are quite interesting and admirable in many respects."

"I don't think there is anything admirable about the Arabs!"

"What a silly thing to say! Whilst Europe was stuck in the Middle Ages, science and the arts were flourishing in the Arab world, restoring Greek values that in Europe were being trampled on or had been forgotten."

"Jewish people have always had thinkers and artists of world stature!"

"But that is not what we are discussing!"

Helena realised that she was talking to a Jewish fanatic and that he was also a little drunk. She tried not to argue any more but to withdraw. However, faced with the continuing absurd comments that he carried on making, she remarked, "The fact is that, whether you like it or not, both peoples live here and they both have to learn to live together without carrying on killing one another."

"That will never be possible because they have already spilt Jewish blood; and you must know that if you or anyone kills one of mine, then I shall kill not one, but a hundred or a thousand of yours," he replied in a very excited state, opening his large, sunken eyes still wider.

"That stupid way of thinking has to change. Humanity has spent centuries trying to find out how to co-exist in a harmonious civilised way: read Plato, Aristotle, Rousseau and others. To argue the way you are doing is to return to the Stone Age."

She had hardly finished saying this when the man got up from the table, shouted something in Hebrew (which Helena couldn't understand) and gave her a resounding slap. Helena reacted instinctively; she picked up the cup of coffee and threw it in his face just as he was clearly getting up to hit her again. At that moment, a young man punched Helena's interrogator in the stomach, leaving him slumped over the table, winded. Sheer terror rooted her to the spot as she surveyed the scene; nevertheless, the young man took her hand and dragged her quickly out of the café.

"Thank you so much," Helena managed to say at last, once they were a few metres away from the cafe.

The young man finally stopped. He saw the look of shock on Helena's face and couldn't help smiling a little at the same time as their eyes met unconsciously for a few seconds. They silently contemplated each other for an instant, which seemed an eternity. He was still a little agitated but, still smiling, he spoke to her as if he had known her all his life. "You must be mad! How on earth can you get into an argument with a drunk who obviously belongs to some extreme organisation. I was sitting at a nearby table, and I was very amused listening to the rationality of your arguments and the incoherence and irrationality of his. Right, I can laugh about it now, but being on your own could have been quite dangerous. Well, what's your name?"

"Helena, and yours?"

"Nadav."

They went on chatting as they walked. She briefly told him how she had come to Israel, as well as about her studies in England.

"What a coincidence! Next month I'm going to Cambridge for a year-or-so as part of an exchange programme between the Weizmann Institute and the University of Cambridge."

"If the Weizmann Institute is in Tel Aviv, what are you doing in Jerusalem?"

"My parents live here so I come regularly to visit them."

"What are you studying?"

"I have a doctorate in mathematics and I am studying plasmas, although my plasmas are astrophysical and not biological like the ones that you know."

They kept on talking as they walked along. They stopped at a Hebrew restaurant to have a meal and continued to enjoy each other's company. Amongst the subjects that they discussed, the one concerning Israel and Palestine was not left out, and Helena commented on the ambiguous image which she had formed of the country. "It has admirable things but, in some ways, it makes me feel ashamed, almost disgusted."

Nadav listened to her quietly, adding, "You are right, but you shouldn't think that all Israelis are like the drunken fanatic who hit you. I myself belong to a sandwich generation; I'm a *tzabarim*, which means born in Israel. My parents emigrated from Poland before the Second World War and formed part of the *Ha Palmaj*, the shock troops of the *Haganah*, the biggest clandestine movement against the British mandate. During the holocaust all our relatives were murdered in Europe in ghettos and concentration camps. My parents took part, as well, in the wars of 1948, 1967 and 1973, and have been active politically, first in the *Mapai* party and then in the Rafi when it was led by David Ben Gurion. For them Israel meant the last hope of finding somewhere to live in peace, free from any further persecution and discrimination. It is easy for me to understand the strong bond that unites my parents and their generation to this place, where there have been so many sacrifices and so much blood. However, many of us young people realise that, paradoxically, the Palestine people have also been victims, indirectly, of the Jewish holocaust in Europe, and ironically the Jews are their executioners; but what else could we have done? Continue with the diaspora in order to go on being victims of discrimination and prejudice? I, like many other Israelis, want a peaceful solution and to establish a respectful co-existence with the Palestinians. However, so much war, so much hate, so much blood and so much suffering have polarised the two sides. I recognise that at times they don't listen to the calls for peace and reason, and I am convinced that we, the younger generation, shall be the ones who have to find a solution to the problem."

When they had finished their meal, Nadav accompanied her to her hotel. On the way, Helena described her life in Cambridge and her experiences as a research student. Nadav listened attentively, staring at her with his steel-grey eyes. Time had flown by. It was almost two in the morning when they reached the hotel and they had been together for almost eight hours, which seemed no time at all to them. At the entrance of the hotel, their thoughts far away, they looked at each other in silence, not knowing what else to say. Slowly, their faces moved closer and – in something that in its tenderness seemed more like the prelude to a caress than the caress itself – scarcely touching, they kissed.

"Thanks for everything," said Helena at last.

"I'd like to thank you. I'll look you up as soon as I get to Cambridge."

Helena watched him disappear through the tenuous light of the moon and some yellowish lamps. She went into her room feeling happy and slept for a few hours, as she would be getting on the Tel Aviv bus very early and then catching the plane to London. In the morning, just as she was handing in her keys at reception on her way out of the hotel, they handed her a rose with an envelope containing a note which she opened anxiously, "We'll meet again in Cambridge. Nadav."

On the plane she found herself sitting next to a middle-aged American who, in a friendly though insistent way, tried to engage her in conversation. At first Helena, who was very distracted, didn't take much notice of what he was saying until he mentioned that he had emigrated to Israel two years ago but was now returning permanently to the United States.

"Of course," he said, "how do you think I feel when my eight-
and eleven-year-old daughters come home from school saying that
Arabs must be killed because they're bad?"

*****

Helena arrived in Cambridge to find the flat empty. Nancy had
returned to the United States and James was on holiday. Early the
following morning she went to the institute to carry on with her work.
She took advantage of the quiet, as several research students and
undergraduates were away, and began to write two articles based on
the results that she had obtained over the previous few months. Back
at the flat in the evening, she wrote to her family and friends, telling
them about her stay in Israel. In fact, apart from a few friends and
members of her family, she didn't write letters to many people
because she had very little free time at her disposal, and because
writing to those close to her tended to depress her. It was also
because, more than once, out of a feeling of obligation, she had
written to relatives or friends who weren't so close telling them about
a visit to a concert, or describing some aspect of her life in
Cambridge. She had received paternalistic and authoritarian replies in
which they reminded her that she had not gone to England to go to
concerts or to take trips into the English countryside, but to study.
This had annoyed her very much as it had been her intention to tell
them something that might have been interesting for them and not to
dwell upon her monotonous daily existence, composed of ten or up to
sixteen hours of work daily, sometimes eating badly and sleeping
badly.

One evening, ten days after she had returned from Israel, she got
back to the flat to find a postal package by the door. It contained a
book and a cassette, but there was no note. However, as she flicked
through the pages she found a message near the beginning which read,
"I hope you like it. Nadav."

Her heart started pounding and, with the book clasped to her
bosom, she lay down to daydream and think of Nadav and how she
had met him. She recalled his angular features, his dark brown hair,
his steel-grey eyes and, of course, his lips and the caress that was

almost a kiss, or rather the kiss that was almost a caress – and also the way in which he gazed so deeply at her. She put the cassette on and listened to Rachmaninov's "Piano Concerto No. 2". She started reading the book which contained a selection of twenty stories by contemporary Israeli authors, most of whom she had never heard of, except for M. Shamir and Amos Oz, from whom she had read very good prose.

Shortly, James returned to the flat with a new tenant, a very shy English girl called Johanna who was an art student and liked cooking Indian food. All three of them quickly struck up a harmonious relationship.

One day, while she was on her own at her work station at the institute finishing an article on the computer, the door opened; it was Nadav holding a bunch of roses. They had been so eager to meet again that as soon as they saw each other they flew into each other's arms. Helena finished printing out her article and then showed Nadav round the institute whilst explaining the experiments that she was conducting. In the evening they went out for a walk and had a meal in a pub. The following day Nadav showed her the small but very pleasant flat that he had rented, and then they went off together to choose a piano for Nadav to hire. In fact, Helena would never have thought it could be so cheap to hire a piano. When she heard him play the various pianos available in order to select one, she was impressed by his skill.

"You told me that you could play the piano, but I never thought that you could play so well."

"It's because I practise ten or twenty minutes every day. Of course, I started learning when I was seven, and I have been playing for twenty years. In fact, it has become a kind of therapy; it helps me relax and feel good. When I don't play for whatever reason, I feel jumpy and irritable."

They visited the Institute of Mathematics where Nadav was going to work. "It's a shame there aren't many laboratories to show you. For my work I only need paper, pencil and sometimes a computer."

They met again at the weekend when Nadav came round very early to take Helena out. "Just look what I've bought!" he shouted through the window, "a second-hand bicycle. Let's go for a ride in the country!"

These first few days Nadav was fascinated by the marked contrast between Israel and England in so far as climate and landscape were concerned.

"I have a surprise for you," said Nadav when they got back. "I have two tickets for a concert in London tonight to hear one of the greatest pianists in this century, Sviatoslav Richter, playing Beethoven's 'Sonata Opus 111'. You'll come with me, won't you?"

"Of course."

"I have still got a lot of things to sort out in my office and in the flat; I'll call for you at six o'clock."

Nadav turned down her offer of breakfast and rode off happily on his bicycle. As arranged, they caught the train to London. During the journey Nadav talked passionately about music and interpretation by pianists whilst Helena looked on attentively and tenderly.

They held hands throughout the concert and Helena saw that tears were rolling down Nadav's cheeks during the *adagio* movement of the "Arietta".

"I thoroughly enjoyed the concert, but I must confess that it wasn't one of Beethoven's compositions that I knew," Helena commented over dinner.

"That's a comment you often hear, especially about his last sonata. I have many friends who are music-lovers who, in spite of being very knowledgeable, seldom get it right when I play them a passage from the 'Sonata Opus 111' (without telling them what it is) and ask them to identify the composer – or at least to tell me in which century it was composed. The most interesting thing is that practically everybody judges it to be twentieth century: they think of Stravinsky, Prokofiev,

Scriabin, and they collapse on the floor when I tell them that they are listening to Beethoven.   This is what I find so fascinating about the music of Beethoven – and I know of no other composer that has it. You can listen to Bach, Handel, Mozart, Schubert, Scriabin or anyone else – both their early and late music – and although there are certain differences, in essence their music still belongs unmistakably to a particular epoch.

"However, this does not apply to Beethoven's music as we can listen to some of his earliest works and be reminded of Haydn and Mozart, or to some of his latest and think of Prokofiev or Schoenberg. This means we are talking about a composer whose music spans a period of more than two centuries.   If we take this exceptional clairvoyance as a starting point to measure the genius of a composer, then there is definitely not, nor has there ever been, anybody who could even be compared to Beethoven.   He took composition to lengths unimaginable in his day.   Astonishingly, the first part of the 'Sonata Opus 111' contains passages that, without any doubt whatsoever, Louis Armstrong would envy, and the final *adagio* is just pure metaphysics, with transformations and transfigurations of the theme until it reaches cosmic spaces and transports us into infinity, to the mystical state that Goethe called *der Fall nach oben*.   It is simply the transformation of temporal existence into atemporal eternity; it is touching and arresting what Plato called "the changeable image of eternity", which is time.   When we get back to Cambridge I'm going to play some variations on the piano for you, such as Nos. 19 and 32, but especially No. 28 of Beethoven's 'Opus 120', which are all indescribably beautiful and innovative, especially for their time as well as ours.   Although, instead of playing it, I suggest listening to a good recording such as that of Claudio Arrau or Sviatoslav Richter."

Helena had been so enraptured that she had not stopped looking at him and listening to him speaking so passionately; her only response was to say that she would be delighted, whilst Nadav poured a bit more *Beaujolais* into their glasses.

Once back in Cambridge they went to Nadav's flat.   While he opened a bottle of *Bordeaux*, Helena took out two glasses and put on Rachmaninov's "Second Piano Concerto".

"Ah, that's the one I sent you! Do you like it?"

"I listen to it every day – I love it; it reminds me of you."

They stood close together and toasted each other.

"To you." said Helena.

"To us."

They sipped the wine and their eyes met. They stayed like that, seeing the universe in each other's eyes. They put their glasses to one side, gently but nervously took hold of each other's hands as their faces moved closer until they dissolved in a seemingly eternal kiss. They caressed each other's back, neck, hair – their anxious bodies, for fear of getting lost or disappearing, were searching and finding each other again in this eternal kiss.

Helena could feel that the button of her dress at the back of her neck was open and that Nadav was caressing her even more passionately and tenderly until she was naked – whilst kissing the lobes of her ears, her neck and her breasts. They lay on the sofa, kissing frantically, delirious with happiness and passion, until gradually Helena felt that he was entering her body.

"I love you, Helena."

"I love you, Nadav."

Something like a whisper could be heard, like a murmur in eternity, between the two bodies that were struggling desperately to be united.

Dawn broke as they went on making love, insatiably.

"I love you, but I was afraid to tell you. I was afraid that you wouldn't believe me."

"I felt the same. I was afraid that you wouldn't believe me because everything had apparently happened so quickly."

"Thank goodness things are as they are now. I couldn't have courted you in the traditional sense of the word. Ever since I got you out of that café in Jerusalem and our eyes met, I have had an indescribable feeling that only now I can understand – I am so lucky; I found you like a teardrop in a forgotten book."

They spent the whole day together, looking at each other and kissing at every moment and loving each other more and more. In the evening Nadav played Bach's "Goldberg Variations" on the piano, with Helena listening, very moved, at his side; then, after dinner, they made love again all night.

Early the next morning, Helena woke up in his arms. She felt so happy that she didn't dare move for fear of waking him, and murmured to herself, "…for love that lets us see others as they are seen by the divine."

When he opened his eyes and saw her gazing at him so tenderly, he could only say, "Do you know that your look is writing worlds in infinity – Aragon would say, *Tes yeux sont si profonds que J'y perds la mémoire.*"

They had breakfast and set out together to work in their respective institutes. At dinner time they met each other again.

"Helena, after dinner we have to go to your flat to get your cases."

This they did, and once settled in Nadav's flat they made love madly.

i like my body when it is with your

body. It is so quite new a thing.

Muscles better and nerves more.

i like your body. i like what it does,

i like its hows. i like to feel the spine

of your body and its bones, and the trembling

-firm-smoothness and which i will

again and again and again

kiss, i like kissing this and that of you,

i like, slowly stroking the, shocking fuzz

of your electric fur, and what-is-it comes

over parting flesh... And eyes big love-crumbs,

and possibly i like the thrill

of under me you so quite new

Nadav soon adopted some of Helena's ways, like going out jogging every day for thirty or forty minutes. They were so happy that they didn't notice time passing. They had already been together for three months, and yet it only seemed like three days. Apart from their academic work, that time had been spent going for walks, going to concerts and making love.

In the evenings, Nadav played the piano for a while, and Helena grew to enjoy Handel, Beethoven, Prokofiev and Schoenberg as much as Mozart and Vivaldi.

"Just listen to this *suite* by Handel – it's absolutely delightful. The same thing happened to poor Handel with his work for 'Klavier' that happened to Beethoven with his 'Lieder'. He was so famous and renowned for his great operas and oratorios that some of his less monumental works, such as his 'Suites für Klavier', were ignored. Just as in the case of Beethoven, his concertos, sonatas and symphonies are such grandiose works that his 'Lieder' have lain forgotten, in spite of the fact that many people who criticise them would be incapable of distinguishing between a Beethoven 'Lieder' and one by Schubert. To set Goethe or Schiller to music, as Beethoven did, is much more difficult than setting poems to music like the ones that Schubert and others selected. You know, as a whole, I adore the work of Bach perhaps as much as that of Beethoven, but if I compare Handel's *suites* with Bach's 'Well Tampered Klavier', then I think I prefer the former, as they are so melodious – however, Bach is more profound."

They spent entire nights, score in hand, listening to the interpretation of either a concerto or a sonata.

"You must be able to say that you like one interpretation more than another because you can distinguish and appreciate the subtleties and often notable differences in execution, as well as the effect that it produces deep inside you. Let's do an experiment. Without your seeing the record sleeves, we shall listen to four different interpretations of the first movement of Beethoven's 'Sonata Opus 31, No. 2, der Sturm'. Would you prefer to listen with or without the score?"

"With the score, so that we can detect the differences more easily."

"Beware, Helena, it's dangerous to be so purist. The score is only a guide and not an inflexible rule. Otherwise, what could the pianist contribute?"

For a while each day when she got home, Helena listened to a little of Prokofiev's piano works in the complete edition of G. Sandor that belonged to Nadav.

"You know, after listening to Prokofiev's music for piano and the last works of Beethoven, as you recommended, I can now see the way in which the former is the spiritual continuation of the latter. If you listen to the rhythm of, for example, Beethoven's 'Variation 17, Opus 120', and that of Prokofiev's 'Toccata Opus 11', not to mention his Sonatas 'Opus 82' and 'Opus 83', it seems to me that if Beethoven had lived a little longer he might have written them himself."

They were both fortunate in having the opportunity of hearing, in London, Prokofiev's 'Sonata Opus 83', superbly interpreted by the talented young Ivo Pogorelich. His performance of "The Precipitato" turned out to be quite masterly since, despite being very loud at the beginning, the piano seemed to burst with the incredible volume, virtuosity and passion of the playing as he reached the *fortissimo* passages at the end.

"If God really does exist, that is where His energy and spirit lie," exclaimed Nadav, commenting enthusiastically upon the interpretation. "Talking of God, I have certainly not seen in you any religious inclination, neither have you asked me if I have any."

"It has always seemed clear to me that you were either an atheist or a lapsed believer. After I'd seen close up in Israel, the hate, irrationality and intolerance that religious fanaticism can lead to, I could not expect anything else."

"You are right. I believe in God, but I refuse to associate Him with any formal religious belief. What about you?"

"I am an atheist, although more through conviction than proof. By that I mean that I start from the premise that it is not possible to prove whether God does or does not exist. However, I must make it clear that by 'God' I understand exclusively the creative entity of the universe and not – as many people understand – an entity that, as well as being the creator of the universe, dictates moral or ethical laws and judges our behaviour. In my opinion, the most pedestrian study in anthropology or the history of human civilisation can make it clear that the latter is only a fine product of the imagination. Ethical norms and rules of moral conduct have always been dictated to suit the groups in power at any point in history. For example, neither you nor I think that slavery is good or just, but how do you think an ancient Greek would respond if we were to ask him for his opinion? And, to cite another example, the Macedonians considered it fine for a young girl to be made love to and to sleep with a man before getting married, and repulsive if it happened after marriage; whereas, for the Greeks, both before and after were equally loathsome. Another very interesting example is that of the Masagetas who, when their progenitors died, cut up their bodies and ate them, as they considered it very beautiful to be entombed in their own children. If we try to see things from their angle, I believe it is a very beautiful and poetic idea – you only have to think that other people burn or bury their dead, even their progenitors. Do you see? Buried or burnt, as if they were waste matter or rubbish. How ungrateful! Whereas a Masageta, in a sublime act of humanity, returns to the depths of his own being, those who gave him life, thus completing a vital cosmic circle. Don't you agree? After all, these are nothing more than examples of cultural relativity, and that is why I only conceive of God as a creative entity without any other attributes. Let's say, like Bernard Shaw, that I have cast off the subordination of heaven."

"So why, when considering whether God the creator does or does not exist, do you prefer to believe that He does not?"

"Because I hate dogmas, and to accept them without question is equivalent to believing that beyond a certain point one can no longer comprehend. In my opinion the greatest possession a human being has is precisely his ability to question, his capacity to wonder at the world and to question everything. To accept a dogma is to commit a crime against the universe, and to believe in God is to accept a dogma."

"Of course, you will already have noticed the circular nature of your reasoning. You hate dogmas, but you do have a dogma, which is not to accept dogmas."

"Yes, I know, but if I have to choose between this or any other dogma, I prefer this one – or perhaps," she added with a smile, "I should prefer to believe that God exists and we do not. Nevertheless, I have to say that the idea of a God is one of the most lovely and poetic that I can imagine; it is the product of an ignorant and defenceless animal, terrified before the infinity of the universe. In fact, Kipling, who was an atheist, wrote a poem called 'Hymn to Physical Pain' in which he gives thanks to God, and he does it because there, poetically, it is required of him. That idea is so beautiful that poetically it is irreplaceable. Doubtless, to have created the idea of God is one of Man's most human and beautiful demonstrations of poetry."

"As you have already said, in my case it's possible to justify religious indifference because of the fanaticism of the atmosphere in which I lived, but you have lived in an almost totally Catholic country."

"A country with a lot of fanaticism and religious violence as well," interrupted Helena. "In fact, my family has suffered directly from fanaticism. My father was a lawyer in a town in the centre of the country where they always accused him of being a mason or a communist although he was neither, just a concerned liberal intellectual who founded, along with other like-minded people, the primary and secondary schools in the town, convinced that education was the best weapon against abuse and injustice. When my mother went out shopping one day, she returned home saying that the central square of the town, next to the town hall and the cathedral, was full of soldiers who had spent the night there. My father, as usual, went off to the town hall to see to some business, but when he reached the square he noticed some men, women and soldiers talking in low voices and glancing over at him. As he went into the town hall, the colonel who was in charge in the square intercepted and asked him to accompany him for questioning. There my father found out why the military detachment had been sent. The priests had spread a rumour that my father, together with other 'communists' and with the support of the 'bearded Cubans' (in fashion at that time because they had just completed their revolution) were ready to take over the cathedral and all the other churches in the town. In order to prevent this and 'to defend themselves from the communists', they had armed the children from the town's religious schools with stones and cudgels. When the rumour reached the military command, they decided to send troops in order to avoid a massacre. Once they had ascertained the truth, the colonel took on the responsibility of severely reprimanding the priests of the town."

Nadav listened in astonishment to Helena's story. "It's quite incredible; it seems like fiction."

"In Mexico in the twenties, a very cruel religious war took place called the *guerra cristera*. I knew old friends of my father, teachers in rural schools at the time, whose tongues and ears were cut off, which is what the *cristera* gangs used to do to their 'enemies'. In my opinion all this is nothing more than a dramatic demonstration of the consequences of ignorance, obscurantism and fanaticism. In fact, the colonel, who on that occasion met my father and who finally became a close friend of his, took an active part in the *guerra cristera*, and to listen to him reminisce was rather dreadful. What was worse was that, after the incident for almost three years, we went every weekend to visit my maternal grandparents who lived in a neighbouring village about a hundred kilometres away. For me as a little girl, it was great fun until I was older, and I found out that because of the rumour spread by the priests of the town – that my father was a 'communist sent by the devil' – he had had virtually no work during those three years, and the weekly visits to my grandparents were to receive money to support us."

Daily life for Nadav and Helena continued to be divided between passionate love, music, reading, work and thirty minutes' jogging, which soon became an obsession – so much so that they decided to train to take part in the London Marathon. At the weekends when they used to go for long bicycle rides in the country, they were now going on equally long running trips but without bicycles.

"Running long distances is really an extremely erotic activity."

"That had never occurred to me."

"Of course," Nadav went on, "it requires a continuous and prolonged physical effort that you must administer carefully if you want to be successful. I must tell you that when I am running I only think about you, so I don't notice the time."

"What other sport have you practised that you have felt equally passionate about?"

"Eight years ago, when I was nineteen, I had the opportunity to go to Switzerland and do a little climbing. Ever since, I have thought that there is no sport that I admire more. There are no spectators or fans applauding like in a stadium, nor are there judges to hand over trophies or medals. You are alone, confronting nature between peaks and precipices, and the only thing that changes is the challenge to yourself, the innate challenge of Man before the universe that surrounds him, the same thing that took him to the poles, to the summit of Everest, to the depths of the oceans and to the moon, and will certainly take him further each time. The sensation of scaling a mountain and seeing the view from the summit is indescribable. Finally, I believe that I love mountaineering as much as I love Bach. Both are sublime human demonstrations of the search for perfection. The difference is that with mountaineering you pay for imperfection with your life."

One Saturday afternoon they set off for London. The following day they were going to run in the marathon. They decided to take their time looking for a hotel where they could sleep and get ready without rushing for the run on Sunday morning. They were on the train in an empty compartment, their heads resting against each other, when suddenly the door opened and in came someone whom they both immediately recognised: it was Vicente, the author of this book. "How are you feeling? Are you ready for the run?"

"We feel a little apprehensive. It's forty-two kilometres and the last few days have been very hot."

"You shouldn't worry. There's a great myth about the marathon – yet any healthy person who, without feeling strain, can run for three or four hours, can run it without any problem. I once ran in the Berlin Marathon. At first I was really afraid that I was not going to be able to finish it, but I managed to come in 1000th, and considering that there were ten thousand runners I was very pleased – no doubt I trained the same as you."

After saying that, Vicente, feeling moved, watched them in silence. He found it difficult to recall a more tender image than that projected by Helena and Nadav. Still looking at them, lovingly and paternally, he took out a book and before leaving the compartment offered it to them. "I hope you enjoy it; it is only to remind you about something that some contemporary writers have forgotten: the burlesque nature of literature."

Helena took hold of it; it was *Altazor* by Huidobro. She read a few lines chosen at random and fell asleep in Nadav's arms:

Hay que resucitar las lenguas

Con sonoras risas

Con vagones de carcajadas

Con cortacircuitos en las frases

y cataclismo en la gramática

Levántate y anda.

[We've got to resuscitate the tongues

With sonorous roars

With wagon loads of laughter

With short circuits in the sentences

and cataclysm in the grammar

Get up and walk]

After the run, they decided to visit museums and in the evening go to a Mozart concert. On the train back to Cambridge, they talked. "Although you play the movements from some of Mozart's sonatas and concertos, I have never heard you speak so enthusiastically about Mozart as you do about Beethoven or Bach. Why not?"

"I am fascinated by Mozart and Vivaldi. For me, as for you, theirs was the music I grew up with, and I still acknowledge the purity and exquisiteness of this music – it's like hearing a child talking. The trouble is that a spirit that can be satisfied just with the conversation of a child is, in my opinion, equally infantile. As I matured, as a man and as a lover of music, I began experiencing stronger and deeper feelings that only Beethoven and Prokofiev could penetrate."

"Before I met you I would have found it difficult to share your point of view, but not now. I should certainly like to ask you a question that for some time has been intriguing me. Which of the various recordings of Beethoven's last sonata for piano, 'Opus 111', do you prefer and why?"

"My reply will seem ingenuous to you, but up to now I have not found one better than any other, in spite of all the discussions about techniques of interpretation I have had over the years. There are such vehement performances like that of Pogorelich, in which what I admire is the extraordinary strength and vitality of the playing. However, there is a performance of this sonata by Claudio Arrau which unfolds before me as I listen to it, a world which is unfathomable and magic in feeling, in a way that no other pianist has achieved. Without realising it, this performance moves me to tears. In spite of it being the same sonata, the emotions and feelings that I experience, depending upon the pianist, can change totally. Without any doubt, the most human and sublime performance of Beethoven's 'Sonata Opus 111' that I have heard is performed by Claudio Arrau. This sonata, which I consider to be the greatest work composed for solo piano by Beethoven, opens doors upon unimaginable universes when played by Arrau."

*****

Helena also felt happy in her work. She had now published five international articles and was preparing to write her doctoral thesis. Together, she and Nadav had planned the future: they had decided to travel to Mexico together. Helena was interested in going back to her country; whereas for Nadav it was all the same wherever he was, as he felt himself to be stateless. Helena had given him an impressive number of books to read on Mexican history, art and culture.

Close to the time when Helena was finishing her doctoral thesis, Nadav received an invitation to take part in a congress in Berlin. They were delighted by the idea of travelling, which for Helena would be a week-long break and an opportunity to get to know the city.

In Berlin they stayed at a small hotel in Kurfüsten Street which suited Nadav fairly well as it was situated close to the centre of the city and was relatively close to the *Philharmonie,* where they had gone to buy tickets for a concert as soon as they arrived in Berlin.

In the mornings, while Nadav attended the congress, Helena visited museums, libraries and places of interest like the Dahlem Museum, the Noue National Galerie or the municipal house of Schönenber. When Nadav saw the museum catalogues, he insisted that they go again, as he didn't want to return to England without seeing them.

That evening they attended the opera where *Romeo and Juliet* awaited them with music by Prokofiev. The introduction was marvellous, and Helena found that Shakespeare's famous tragedy, written in 1595, had had a very chequered and long history that had begun in Italy in 1476, when Masuccio Salernitano wrote *L'historia di Marlotto e Giannozza*; then, after several transformations, it had moved on to France where it inspired Pierre Boaistuau to write his *Histoires Tragiques* in 1559; from there it went to Spain, to England and finally to Germany. In Spain, Lope de Vega, in 1602, presented it as *Castelvines y Monteses*; in England, Arthur Brook wrote *The Tragicall Historye of Romeus and Juliet* in 1562, which is the direct antecedent of the *Romeo and Juliet* of Shakespeare, and in Germany,

Philip Harsdorfer wrote *Die verzweifelte Liebe* in 1615. It is to say that, amongst the twenty-or-so versions of the same story, it is Shakespeare's that is the most well known nowadays. It interested them to learn, at the same time, of the existence of more than thirty different musical productions and librettos written for the operatic representation of this tragedy, including the one performed in Mexico in 1863 with the music of Melesio Morales and the libretto of Felice Romani.

They also went to the Gropius Museum and to the new museum next to it in the Prinz-Albrech-Terrain, in what were the cells and dungeons of the central offices of the secret state police, the *Gestapo*, and the squadrons of protection, the *Schutzstaffel*, known as the SS. That, for both of them – particularly for Nadav – was very impressive. The collection of informative state papers, *Relchsgesetzblat*, and the official newspapers of the epoch like *Der Angriff* and the *Volkischer Beobachter*, made the unbelievable argument of "ignorance", according to which the German people "did not know what was happening." Helena's attention was drawn to the text of the "Law for the protection of German blood and German honour" from the 15th of September, 1935, where in its fourth article it states: "1st: Every Jew is forbidden to use the national flag or to show the national colours. 2nd: They can, however, show the Jewish colours; the right to do this will be guaranteed by the State."

"Of course, in that way they could locate them more easily," said Nadav.

"All this is so incredibly absurd. This article in particular reminds me of a Mexican labour law issued during the *porfiriato* which obviously did not entertain any idea of the workers having effective labour rights but, on the other hand, at some point said, 'However, if a worker is not satisfied with his work, he has the right to hand in his notice whenever he likes.'"

"It is a shame," commented Nadav, "that Nazi ideas about the German race have still not disappeared. In fact, they continue to be in force in various clauses of German legislation. Like the case of the Romanian, now 'German', that we met in the hotel. I wonder how it is possible that a person who has proved that he has German ancestry going back five generations receives, just for that, German nationality despite the fact that he has never lived there, has never contributed to the socio-economic development of the country and knows absolutely nothing about the German language and culture. Meanwhile, the third and fourth generations who are the direct descendants of Turkish workers, who have given their strength, their sweat, and a strong economic contribution to the construction of this country, and who don't even know the Turkish language or customs since they have been brought up in Germany, cannot obtain German nationality. And this reflects the idea still prevailing, that 'Germanhood' is something immutable, that it is in the blood and that that is what distinguishes them from the rest."

"You are right. You see, during the time you have spent at the conferences, I have had the opportunity to chat with several Germans, and what surprised me was that although a high percentage of the people that I have met condemn nazism, fascism and racism; in their opinions about different economic and social themes, they adhere faithfully to these positions. Just today, a German – an older man – asked me how it could be that in Mexico and Latin America there was so much poverty. I gave him a general idea about the historical development of the region and in particular, that of Mexico. I gave him information that he did not know: the three hundred years of Spanish colonisation – and in parenthesis I have to tell you that, in my opinion, this Spanish inheritance constitutes the origin of a large portion of Mexico's evils – likewise I told him about the wars of the last century against Spain, France and the United States that left the country bankrupt, ending the century with a dictatorship and initiating this one with a revolution followed by a religious war. In conclusion, the reasonably stable development of Mexico has been for just the last few decades. The German explained to me how the Second World War had totally destroyed Germany but that, in spite of everything, they had rebuilt it. Looking at his blue eyes, smiling and overbearing, I came to the conclusion that he wanted me to understand that if in Mexico and Latin America we are poor, it is because of the innate characteristics of the inhabitants and nothing else. I replied that he should not forget that in the rebuilding of Germany after the Second World War, a large part of the credit should go to the United States that, through the Marshall Plan, gave economic aid, and also to the Turkish workers who provided labour at a very low cost. I think that this last point must have displeased him very much because without saying another word he turned around and walked off."

*****

Nadav had managed to get tickets at the *Philharmonie* for that evening. The main part of the programme consisted of Beethoven's "Concerto Opus 58", interpreted by Vladimir Ashkenazy. As soon as they went inside, they felt their skin tingle.

"Isn't it magnificent!" whispered Nadav.

"This place has the solemnity of a temple. What I feel here is only comparable to what I have felt visiting great cathedrals," commented Helena.

"For many it is the world temple of music."

The performance could be declared brilliant. When they left they walked along until they came to a *Kneipe* and went in to have a beer.

"The only thing that seems incredible to me, truly incredible, is the musical ignorance and lack of respect of the audience: applauding between movements and taking photographs during the performance!"

"Yes, I must admit I never expected to see that. Although, one must not forget that tourists form a large part of the audience."

"That's no justification. In London as well there were many tourists present, and the reverence and the exemplary behaviour of the audience bears no comparison with what we have seen here."

"I propose we forget about that and instead toast the performance."

Laughing and chatting, they each drank about four beers and then, arm in arm, they took a little stroll around Berlin by night, taking in its beauty and its charms.

The following day they met at lunch time. Helena showed him a beautiful edition of Goethe's *Faust* that she had bought, as well as the latest novel by Kundera. "Now that I am about to finish my doctorate and have re-read the first words pronounced by Faust, I think I understand his message better than ever. Listen to this:

Habe nun, ach! Philosophie

Juristerei und Medizin

Und Leider und Theologie

Durchaus studiert, mit heiBem Bemühn

Da steh ich nun, ich armer Tor,

Und bin so klug als wie zuvor!

Hieße Magister, Heiße Doctor gar

Und ziehe schon an die zohen Jahr

Herauf, herab und quer und Krum

Heine Schüler an der Nase herum

Und sehe daß wir nichts wissen können!

"When I finished my doctorate I certainly felt as you do now."

*****

At the conference, Nadav met a very agreeable Mexican professor whom he knew through his scientific articles – which were exemplary for their sharpness and imagination – and they arranged to go out for dinner together. "Helena, let me introduce you to your compatriot, Professor Sánchez."

"Pleased to meet you," said Helena in Spanish as they set off.

Professor Sánchez was an older man of about fifty-five who looked intelligent and shrewd, just like his mind. As they went into the restaurant and sat down, he commented, "At all gatherings, Kant always tried to follow the rule of Lord Chesterfield in that the number of fellow diners must be bigger or equal to the number of the Graces and less than or equal to that of the Muses."

In answer to a question Helena had asked him about his professional work, Professor Sánchez outlined very briefly his career as a physicist and his job in Mexico. Helena remarked ingenuously, "I am so pleased to meet a famous Mexican scientist."

"Don't forget that to be famous in Mexico is of no consequence."

"Don't be so modest, Professor. They tell me that at the Weismann Institute in Israel and in Cambridge, each one of your publications is given great attention and discussed."

"Well, is that so?! I am happy to know that my work is not done in vain!"

Helena spent a long time talking enthusiastically about her research in Cambridge and talked about her intention, with Nadav, to go back to Mexico. "What do you think of that idea?" As she asked this question, Helena noticed a certain hesitation in the professor's expression, and so she added, "Please give us your frank opinion."

"If you want it, I shall give it to you simply: don't go back to Mexico. You will have nothing to do there."

"How is it possible for you to say that, having spent the whole of your professional life in the country?"

"Precisely because of that," he answered, staring at her with a slight smile.

Helena was speechless, and in the absence of any comment from her he added, "I have spent thirty years seeing talented young people wasted and frustrated, as well as the creation and failure or destruction of innumerable institutions of science and of higher education in Mexico."

"But they don't need us outside Mexico," interrupted Helena. "If we stay in Europe or the United States, our presence or absence would mean nothing for the scientific development of those countries. Besides that, science and scientific work cannot be thought of as something 'abstract' and removed from Man and society. As far as I am concerned, I feel a strong moral obligation to return to Mexico. I see that I am its social product, a result of the enormous efforts of a third-world country in which thousands of workers, who already earn for themselves miserable 'minimum salaries', are taxed to pay for the construction of universities, to give grants to students, to pay teachers and to undertake an enormous number of tasks – however incomplete and inefficient these are in a complicated socio-economic network of which I am the result."

"I find it very moving to hear you talk like that because it reminds me of my feelings when I returned to Mexico. The problem is that in the time that has elapsed, I have realised that scientific development in Mexico is something that in reality matters to almost nobody. Worse still, the structure of the country conforms to this in such a way that the failure of whatever scientific intent is guaranteed. Look, we have a government that has for decades dedicated to science and education much lower percentages of GNP than the minimum recommended by international organisations like UNESCO, and if that is not enough, those amounts set aside, already low, have declined sharply in the past few years. To this you have to add serious practical problems like the acquisition of an electric plug that costs a few pesos and requires various purchasing requests, the involvement of at least four to six persons including bosses, secretaries and others, and a period of waiting that can be up to a fortnight. And all this supposing that your research does not require the import of equipment or materials because in that case, periods of waiting can be over two years or even more, and when the equipment reaches Mexico, if it has not been destroyed or stolen by customs, then you have to pay bribes or make use of your 'contacts' in order to get the purchase handed over. I'm not telling you this simply to mention the incredible stupidity and lack of common sense on the part of the bureaucrats, management and administrators of many of the research centres and almost all the institutions responsible for supporting science in Mexico. Cheap politics, tricks and foul play are practised as much by the administrators as by the scientists who have joined in the game, sending scientific interests to the devil for political power and the canonisation of their names. This combination ends up crushing, above all, the youngest members of our community. Add to all that the changes that occur every six years when politicians and administrators, with the object of demonstrating scientific or technological results that are publicly popular and are politically useful to them in currying favour with their superiors, destroy or modify as they please from their desks, projects that could have cost years of effort and dedication on the part of science enthusiasts. I do not know what else I could say to you. I could tell you about shameless excesses, like the heads of some institutes who take home to their families and friends costly equipment to play with that not even you as a researcher have free access to, on the pretext that they must sign some bits of paper to O.K. the stuff – or I could tell you about more serious things like the business of the research institute that, shortly after my return to Mexico a group of us founded in a provincial university, was annihilated with the approval, or perhaps on the orders, of the government. A band of wild idiots armed with sticks was sent to destroy the laboratories, the library and the rest of the installations from which I had to run to get out, literally dodging the missiles."

"So how come you remain in Mexico?" asked Helena, surprised yet serious.

"There was always some project supported by enthusiastic groups that made me think, 'Now we are going to do it,' and in one way or another, in the end nothing came of it, at least nothing in the form in which it had been originally conceived. When I wanted to leave, I realised that it was then too late. Scientists are contracted when they are young and have their potential before them and not when they are older. To what I have said to you, I should add that there is a Mexican scientific prejudice according to which, if you return to Mexico, it is because you are not good enough, as the really good ones stay away. In the end, you might or might not be in agreement with everything that I have said, but there is a fact which nearly every Mexican scientist agrees on, and that is that to be a scientist in Mexico, you need to be essentially a 'romantic masochist'."

That night in the hotel, Helena realised that the conversation with Professor Sánchez had without doubt cast a shadow over her optimism. For his part, Nadav commented, "I don't know Mexico, but I know that I love you, and I am happy to be wherever you want to be. You make the decision. I shall be at your side."

"The trouble is that I no longer know what the best decision is," replied Helena.

Back in England, the most pleasant memory she had of Berlin, apart from the conversation with Professor Sánchez, was the visit that they had made to East Berlin in the company of Joachim, a friendly young German mathematician, whom Nadav had met at the congress, and his intelligent and multilingual wife, Monika. With them they had visited the imposing museum of the Pergamon and spent hours strolling along *Unter den Linden* from the Brandenburg Gates to Alexanderplatz. "We've met some really pleasant and fine people," Helena had exclaimed after the walk.

In Cambridge, Helena had finished her doctoral thesis and was waiting for the date of submission. Nadav received a letter from the Israeli Ministry of Defence, informing him that he should present himself for the two months' annual military service, as his second request for exemption had not been approved. The notice made them feel sad, as Helena was wanting him to be there when she submitted her thesis. "I can't get out of it," said Nadav, sad and annoyed, "I could get myself into very serious problems if I don't obey this call-up order."

They said a sad farewell at Heathrow airport in London. With a lump in their throat and broken-hearted, they embraced for a final kiss. It was the first time that they had been parted in the two years that they had lived together, and they had never imagined that it could be so hard.

Helena submitted her doctoral thesis which was very well received. Now, anxiously, she only waited for Nadav. In the mornings she went out running and during the day read and listened to music – in particular, to Schubert's last sonata that Nadav so loved to play on the piano. *Leipzig, Veerlag von Breitkofp & Härtel, Sonate (in B dur) für das Pianoforte componirt von Franz Schubert (Componirt im September 1828). Molto moderato, pianissimo, legato.* Chords which introduce a gentle and profound melody are brought to a conclusion with a solemn and mysterious trill. The theme is repeated and also the solemn trill. The theme in *crescendo*. The theme in forte. *Descrescendo* and the solemn trill is repeated. And Nadav is far away and the solemn trill is repeated. And Nadav's absence tastes of the light of the moon and the solemn trill is repeated. *Decrescendo, piano, pianissimo, mempre legato.*

The date of Nadav's return passed while Helena's anguish grew with the complete absence of any news. She got up one morning to find a letter in the post box. It was from Israel and she opened it quickly. She was surprised that the handwriting was not that of Nadav, and in English she read the following:

"My dear Helena:

I was a companion of Nadav in the Army where he told me a lot about you. Unfortunately, a few days ago, on a routine mission on patrol, we were attacked and he died instantly. I am so sorry for you and I share your grief ..."

She didn't finish reading it as her eyes were filled with tears. With the letter in her hand and her soul in torment she collapsed ... *and weeping like a rainbow without colours, like a benighted dog howling, like a child who sings sitting on a tear, like a child weeping beside a sigh, like a child who enters the nest of tears, like a giraffe in the middle of the desert grazing, self-absorbed, on the grasses of the moon* ... she stayed there, oblivious to time.

Berlin – Guanajuato, 1990.